Lobos,
Blue Devils, and Mustangs
(A 'Non-Fictional' Fiction)

A Novel By
CEDRIC EDWARDS

Lobos, Blue Devils, and Mustangs – A "nonfictional" Fiction
By: Cedric Edwards

Cover Designed By: Jazzy Kitty Publishing
Cover images: Cedric Edwards
Logo Designs By: Andre M. Saunders
Editor: Anelda L. Attaway

© 2015 Cedric Edwards
ISBN 978-0-9916648-7-0
Library of Congress Control Number: 2015940811

All rights reserved. This book is protected under the copyright laws of the United States of America. This book may not be copied or reprinted for commercial gain or profit. The use of short quotations or occasional page copying for personal or group study is permitted and encouraged. Permission will be granted upon request. For Worldwide Distribution available in Paperback and EBook. Printed in the United States of America. Published by Jazzy Kitty Greetings Marketing & Publishing, LLC dba Jazzy Kitty Publishing. Utilizing Microsoft Publishing Software.

ACKNOWLEDGMENTS/DEDICATIONS

To Aaliyah and Alijah, My grand-babies

Dedicated to the Longview High School (Texas) Class of 1986, The Best Class Ever!

Thanks to God and Jesus Christ, my parents for raising me, my sister, Poinsettia, for being the perfect little sister, my family for supporting me: Loretta, my wife; Brittany and Whitney, my daughters; and my two babies Alijah and Aaliyah; my best friend Dennison for being like a brother to me; my other best friends Marcus, Larry, Reggie, Choyce, and Tonika, and their families for encouraging me constantly and being there for me through thick and thin; my colleagues and co-workers at Longview High School for their encouragement; and last but definitely not least, my classmates and forever friends in the Class of 1986 for being the BEST CLASSMATES a fellow could ever ask for...Without you all, this book would not be possible.

Thank you one and all!

TABLE OF CONTENTS

INTRODUCTION i
CHAPTER 1 – Me and My Buddies... 01
CHAPTER 2 – September to Remember................................... 19
CHAPTER 3 – Back in the Day 41
CHAPTER 4 – Kelly and Me, Part 1 55
CHAPTER 5 – Kelly and Me, Part 2 75
CHAPTER 6 – Devin's Song.. 81
CHAPTER 7 – Changes in November... 88
CHAPTER 8 – Annette and Me 98
CHAPTER 9 – The District Champions 108
CHAPTER 10 – When I Was Young 130
CHAPTER 11 – The Birth of the House Rockers..................... 156
CHAPTER 12 – The Round Table 164
CHAPTER 13 – What is Calculus 173
CHAPTER 14 – The Senior Celebration 184
CHAPTER 15 – A Star is Born.. 195
CHAPTER 16 – No Hablo Espanol, I Just Take It 202
CHAPTER 17 – Kelly and Me, Part 3 215
CHAPTER 18 – Prom Night 86 (Finally!) 230
CHAPTER 19 – The End.. 240
CHAPTER 20 – Graduation 86 (Finally!) 244
ABOUT THE AUTHOR.. 253

INTRODUCTION

Twenty-eight years ago, I graduated from Longview High School in Longview, Texas. 1986 was a GOOD year.

From 1978 to 1986, my friends and I spent our childhood lives trying to be teenagers and make decisions that would culminate in May of 1986 when we received our tickets to freedom by graduating from good 'ol Longview High. Some of the decisions we made were good decisions; some obviously were not. There was a lot of growing up and learning which needed to be done, a *lot* of it! And a lot of funny things happened along the way.

Out of all those years, obviously my senior year would be the most memorable and enjoyable one, and that's the one I chose to remember mainly in this book. I was like every other 17 year-old boy at that time-I thought about girls, football, sports, girls, my grades, going to college, girls, playing dominoes, getting a car, and of course, girls. So you see where my mind was mainly back then. There will be times where I will look back at certain events and things that had occurred in years prior to my senior year, and I would revel in my triumphs and suffer in my defeats. Everything, however, would lead to that final year of high school. This book is a humorous look back at that year and those times based on my real-life experiences.

Lobos, Blue Devils, and Mustangs – A "nonfictional" Fiction is a journey from my elementary school and middle-school years to possibly the greatest year of my life--the year I finished high school.

Cedric Edwards, April 2014.

CHAPTER 1

Me and My Buddies

August, 2013

Twenty-seven years ago, I graduated from Longview High School in Longview, Texas. In the years that followed, I attended college, finished a technical school, got married, worked various jobs, and experienced the highs and lows of becoming an adult. Now, I find myself back at Longview High School for my tenth year working as an instructional assistant/inclusion teacher, and not-so-shockingly, it's been a feeling of deja-vu. You know, like they say, the more things change, the more they stay the same. Or, to look at it from a different perspective, you *can* go home again. Watching and seeing some of my peers' kids walk the same hallways as their parents did, and more often than not, act as their parents did, brought back memories of the times when we were the ones populating the school and driving the teachers and principals insane. Some of us that is. Most of us were actually there to get an education. It might not have just been an education in math and history and the like, but as long as we were getting some sort of education in life itself, I guess that was all right. From 1978 to 1986, my friends and I spent our childhood lives trying to be teenagers and making decisions that would culminate in what was to occur in May of 1986 when we received our tickets to freedom by graduating from good 'ol Longview High. But there was a lot of hard work and a lot of growing up which needed to be done. A *lot* of it. Out of all those years, obviously the last one would be the most memorable and enjoyable one, and that's the one I chose to remember mainly in this book. There will be times where I will look back at certain events and things that had occurred in years prior to my senior year, but everything will come back to that final year of high school. This book is a journey, from my elementary school and middle-school years to possibly the greatest year of my life--the year I finished high school.

Most of the stories you'll read about were based on my real-life experiences, so most (if not all) of this stuff actually happened. I gathered most of my memories from a journal I used to keep back in the day, so there'll be a diary-like feel to this book. But there were also a few instances where I let my imagination and creativity run wild and I came up with some "tall tales". This is why I label my book a "non-fictional fiction". You can figure out for yourself what's true and what isn't. (Have fun!) Of course, names have been changed to protect the innocent as well as the guilty, but the characters are all based on my classmates, friends, and family. Remember, this is truly a fiction, not a "tell-all" book. (Sorry, ex-classmates out there.) And this is a fun(ny) and (very) interesting look back at a time in my life I will never forget. The year 1986 seems today like it occurred 100 years ago rather than 27, but still, it's a memorable year. When our 30th-year class reunion comes up in a few years, maybe I'll give my classmates something to talk about one more time. But then again, maybe I'll put 'em all to sleep if they read this book. (But I doubt it!) Anyway, as with all stories, it's best to start at the *very beginning*:

The First 17 Years: A Summary

What's up? My name is Cedric Edwards and I'm the author of this book. Obviously, I was destined for a strange life from the time I was born. In September of 1968 I was born in a town called Kittery, Maine. It happened to be snowing at the time, so considering I was to spend most of my life in Texas, I guess that might be the only reason I can deal with cold temperatures and sometimes sleep with the air-conditioner on during the *winter*. Anyway my parents and I only lived in Maine for about three months, and then we moved to Longview. My dad was in the Air Force back then, so up until the time I was nine years old, we moved around a lot. So much so that by the time I entered the sixth grade, I had attended *five different elementary schools!* We stayed in Longview for a couple of years (I was a baby so I don't remember anything about that period of time), then we moved to Alamogordo, New Mexico. During the time we lived in New Mexico, I gained a travelling partner in my little sister, Flower, who, being three years younger than I, was at least spared some of the moving around. I usually called her "Flower-child" because she was born in the '70s. (I'm not going to say what she called me, however.)

Speaking of the 1970s, the late 60s and early 70s were a time of change for the United States in general, and my family and I were not immune to the changes. I didn't realize it back then, but we were in the midst of a lot of social and economic changes going on at that time, and the civil rights movements of the 60s had led to a lot of these changes. For instance, there were still segregated schools at the time I was born, and integration for some places didn't take place until 1970. Being black myself and a little kid during this time, I was only acutely aware of the changes. And living for the most part on Air Force bases early on kind of sheltered me from these changes also. But as I grew older and we continued to move, I became more and more aware of my identity, my feelings, and my surroundings, and some of them, I didn't like. Don't get me wrong; I liked going to and visiting different places (I still do), but there were times when the moving and travelling actually bothered me, especially the last couple of times we moved. I hated constantly having to make new friends all over again and being the "new kid on the block" almost every year.

By the time we had moved to Longview for the third and final time after my dad's retirement from the Air Force, I was sick and tired of moving, and I had liked the last place we lived, which happened to be Abilene, Texas. It was a place I did not want to leave. But of course, a nine-year old didn't have much say in where his family was or wasn't going to live (at least not back then), and there was nothing I could do but go. When your dad or mom is in the Air Force or in the armed services period, then you've got to go where and when they tell you to go. Daddy did this for a long period of time--over 20 years, then finally decided to settle down in Longview after his retirement. It could've been worse; my parents were considering living in nearby Marshall or Fort Worth. I can't imagine what that would've been like. And I don't want to, either.

So, for the next seven years, I was a Mustang (Jodie McClure Elementary), a Blue Devil (Judson Middle School), and of course, a Lobo. My *one* year at Jodie McClure was great, the three years at Judson were up and down, and my ninth and tenth grade years at LHS were horrific, to say the least. I suppose all teenagers go through this thing of not understanding their parents and vice versa, but to say my parents and I didn't understand one another or see eye-to-eye during this time would be a huge understatement. It was more like eye-to-toes. And as if my life couldn't be any more miserable at that time, I had to start wearing glasses in middle school and was short and skinny during that time. (I wouldn't start growing physically *and* mentally until I became a junior in high school.) So, obviously, I got picked on half the time and had my share of fights. I wasn't a bad kid, but I thought my parents were just *too* strict. In fairness to them, however, and considering I've had teenagers of my own to raise, if they had not been so strict with my sister and me, we'd probably ended up in jail or something. They did raise us the best they could, and I'm thankful to God for that.

BUT back then I could not see that. If I hadn't put myself in different activities, sports, or clubs at school, I probably would not have gotten to do *anything*. In the ninth and tenth grades, in my parents' house, this is the way it was: Go to school, learn something, go home, study, go to church, act right, go to bed and go to sleep. There wasn't too much of anything else to do unless I went out on my own looking for it. I had many friends and a few close friends whom y'all will be hearing more about in later chapters, but I didn't hang around them a lot outside of school at first. I mostly kept to myself especially during those first couple years of high school.

Then during the second semester of my tenth grade year, I started to change. I realized if I went through my high-school life with my mouth closed every single day, and if I continued to act shy and somewhat unfriendly, I was going to be a very boring and lonely person, and of course, I didn't want that, especially when it came to the opposite sex. Even though I was and still am (kind of) a very shy person (well, maybe not that shy now), incredibly (for me, that is) I started opening up more and being more friendly and outgoing. This metamorphosis had started during the last half of my 10th grade year. Besides my classmates and friends, some of the adults whom I knew a little more than casually really helped me at this time. Coach James, one of my football coaches, and Mr. and Mrs. Homer Queen, my neighbors down the street, were great, positive influences on me. Coach James helped me get back into Athletics at the end of that year, and the Queens kept me from getting too down on myself during the not-so-fun times. We'd play dominoes, and Mr. Queen would have his fun giving me beatings. (But that wouldn't last, of course.) All of this helped me to go from almost becoming an introvert to being someone who actually existed.

My sister and I also spent some time with our Aunt Dee during the summer preceding my junior year. We went to Port Arthur and had an excellent time. We ate all the seafood we wanted, we made a few new friends, and of course I met a girl down there who was kinda nice. In fact, Flower-child and I *didn't* want to come home. We wanted to stay and live with our auntie and go to school there. It's funny, but that was one of the few times I *wanted* to move. But ultimately we were talked out of that and more or less forced to come home. This all led to my great junior year, as the transformation was complete. I had stopped wearing glasses and the ugly clothes my parents wanted me to wear, and started wearing more up-to-date clothes. I even grew my hair long into a curl (No more short haircuts or small afros), and I had more confidence in myself than ever before. I joined a few clubs, I was in football, I made the honor roll every six weeks, and I was more popular than ever before. I wasn't afraid to talk to girls (sometimes), I came to school every day, and everything was great...or was it?

So, in August of 1985, I was preparing for my final year at LHS. I was only in the Spanish Club and in football on the varsity team, and of course Momma wasn't too happy about that. She didn't seem to want me to take part in anything. Over-protective? Yes, definitely. Plus, she also tried to discourage me from talking to girls, telling me to concentrate on my studies more. I was determined to concentrate on my studies *and* talk to girls, whichever came first. (Smile) I also wanted to get my drivers' license, but at that time, my parents were totally against that. I guess they thought I was going to wreck <u>another</u> car. (That's another story for later.) Anyway, I was beginning to see that this was going to be a year where I was going to have to earn almost everything on my own...with a little help from my friends, of course. So I closed my eyes, gritted my teeth, and said to myself, *'Onward, into the abyss....'*

Saturday, August 31, 1985: Prelude

I had two real good friends while in high school who were like brothers to me.

If not for them, I'd *really* been boring. Life would have been boring. This book would be boring to read. (Y'all get the picture.) They, like myself, were going to be seniors, too, so we went through it all together year after year after year. So they, my buddies and true amigos, get a section of this chapter all to themselves.

My best friend for most of my high school years was a guy named Dave Garrison. How we became such good friends is kind of a mystery in itself because we were somewhat different when we first met back in the ninth grade. First, he was white and I was black. (I'm still black, but that's beside the point.) He was way more friendlier than I was, more outgoing, more smarter, more talented, more everything. Really, we should've called him, "Mr. Everything". I was quieter, more to myself, and not very popular. Dave got along with *everybody*, it didn't matter who you was or what you was. He had such a friendly, humble, and winning personality that you would have thought he was the second coming of Mr. Rogers. He would give you the clothes off his back and think nothing of it. I think what made Dave such an easy person to get along with and be friends with was that he was very down-to-Earth. I swear I never saw him upset or mad, and he <u>always</u> had a smile on his face. For real. I'm pretty sure he had problems like the rest of us, but he never showed it.

The first time we met, we had Geometry together, and he sat behind me. (This was to be a common occurrence for the next four years in our classes together.) I remember him saying to someone else that he felt I was going to do real well in that class since I was sitting there minding my own business looking quiet and real studious. (Actually I was trying to be as inconspicuous as possible and trying real hard to concentrate on what Mr. Pear, the teacher, was saying. And not doing too good of a job since I didn't understand Geometry back then and still don't today.) "He looks real smart," he told his friend. (Yeah, I looked smart. Go figure.) Really and truly, he was the one who did *very* well in that class and the one *I* would usually ask for help. And from that beginning, we became very good friends as we learned we had a lot of things in common, from being die-hard Dallas Cowboys fans to thinking about girls a little too much.

I think that out of all my classmates, I had classes with Dave the most, sometimes two or three classes a year. He was probably the smartest guy in our class, and whether or not he realized it, he really helped me a lot with my work intentionally *and* unintentionally. He motivated me to do better by being such a good example (as far as making good grades were concerned, not studying, of course). One moment where I took this to the extreme was when we had English together in the tenth grade. We were supposed to memorize Marc Antony's speech in Julius Caesar for homework and say it out loud the next day in class. For some unknown reason, I had totally forgotten all about it until Dave mentioned it when we walked into class.

"Did you memorize the speech?"

"What speech?" I said densely.

"Marc Antony's speech."

"We were supposed to do that?"

"Yep. We've got to say it today."

"You're kidding."

"Nope."

"Crap."

"You didn't memorize it?"

Heck, I hadn't even *looked* at it. I ran to my desk and threw open the book and found the speech. It looked to be as long as the Old Testament.

Dave seemed to be surprised himself that I hadn't studied and had forgotten about the homework. "What are you going to do?" he asked. "I'm fixing to memorize this thing in record time. Just watch me." Since the teacher was going in alphabetical order according to our last names, there were just four people ahead of me who had to say their speeches, so I figured that gave me about 15 minutes to get the thing memorized. Dave could look at something one time and know it, just like that; *that's* just how smart he was. And I was going to prove that I could do it, too. Of course, I had never done anything like this before; usually I might would just take my zero and go on, but at that moment, I didn't need or want a zero. That would've sent my English grade into the danger zone and me with it as far as my parents were concerned. Dave watched me as I read and re-read it and said it to myself constantly until it was my turn to go up in front of the teacher, and when my turn came, I went up, said a prayer, took a deep breath, and did the impossible:

I said the <u>WHOLE</u> speech, <u>without</u> an error! In record time possibly.

I went back to my desk totally relieved and kind of in shock, almost unbelieving what I had done. Dave *was* SHOCKED, and then he said, "You were tricking me, weren't you? You had me believing you hadn't memorized the speech when you actually did have it memorized. You just wanted to be dramatic and make me think you can memorize that thing in less than fifteen minutes. Didn't you?"

I said, *"Yeah right,"* trying not to shake from being so nervous. This nearly had been more exciting than a football game!

Well, maybe not.

Needless to say, when Dave's turn came, he was still so much in shock that he missed three or four words while saying the speech. "It's your fault," he said when he came back to his desk, "you fouled up my concentration." All I could think was that we had obviously switched places for one day.

Another time, Dave and I decided we were going to be, of all things, the next rap stars. This was during our junior year in school. Never mind that neither one of us had ever rapped before in our lives and never mind that us doing rap would be like the Rolling Stones trying to do opera. Despite all that, we were determined to try anyhow. One thing I liked about Dave, he wasn't afraid to try or do different things, and neither was I, no matter how stupid it was. And this, my friends, this was kind of stupid looking back on it.

Our plan was for me to write the words to the songs and for him to select the music it would go to. At the time, we were really into *Run D.M.C.*, *Whodini, The Fatboys*, and *Zapp*, so our music was to have their influences mostly. Then we would combine the words with the music and attempt to create a rap masterpiece (or pieces) that could someday go to the top of the charts, sell millions, and make us a lot of money. This was all done before karaoke existed, so yeah, it was a good idea while it lasted, but it had some snags in it, of course.

First, as I've mentioned, we had no skills as rappers. I could write good songs (at least, I thought they were good), and Dave could pick out and create some decent music, but as rappers, we were terribly lacking. We were able to put together *one* halfway-decent song (words, music, and rap) and I'd let you hear it except that it's locked in a box that's missing its key, which happens to be locked in a trunk that's also missing its key. And that trunk is way in the back of my closet under a whole bunch of junk. In other words, you wouldn't want to hear the song anyway. It just didn't sound right. We sounded like constipated hogs on crack. Believe you me, it was terrible and terrible-sounding.

Which brings us to the second snag: We didn't have the right equipment. Remember, again this was done before the time of karaoke machines and CDs and DVDs and all that. And since we didn't know anyone with a production studio or anything similar, we had to make due with a tape recorder and microphone and some drumsticks (I don't know what happened to the drums). As I said, it just didn't sound right. Which was probably the understatement of the year, all things considered.

Third, we couldn't really decide on a good name to call ourselves. We finally decided to call ourselves "Rap D.N.C." after Run D.M.C. Our name stood for **Rap**masters **D**ave **N** (and) **C**edric, but obviously, that wasn't very original. Neither was the one song we did, called *"The Rapmasters"* or something like that. All we did was brag on ourselves, saying we were the coolest, the hippest, and so forth and so on. And I hate to say this *again*, even though I was the one who wrote the words, but it just wasn't very good. It was *horrible*. I cringe now just writing about this. After we put the song on tape, we let some of our classmates listen to it, and the reactions ran from uncontrollable laughter to shock to horrified expressions at letting human ears hear something so hideous.

Needless to say, that was the end of "Rap D.N.C." Dave and I decided that the world was not ready for our brand of rap, so we went back to doing normal things like complaining about the Dallas Cowboys and looking at and talking about girls.

Then there was the time Dave got his car, a 1983 Ford Mustang. He was one of the first of my classmates to get a car, so we were all in awe of him and his car. It was dark blue and black, and at the time, to me, the best-looking and best-running car around. So if y'all thought I was a little envious of Dave and his car, well, maybe just a tad bit. I probably loved that car more than he did. BUT I doubt it. (It was close.) Dave loved that car and loved showing it off. He got it midway through our 10th grade year and it wasn't long before he asked me if I wanted to go for a spin with him. I didn't want to sound too excited when I said, *'Sure'*, but it was hard not to. I almost all, but asked him if *I* could drive the car, and I didn't even know how to drive at the time.

The first two things I noticed when we got in was the stereo and sound system and the stick-shift, three things I loved in a car. *Yeah, that's what I'm talking about,* I thought as he started the car, turned up the music, and cut on the AC. And as we roared out of the student parking lot and got on the Loop, everything was operating at top-capacity. We flew down McCann Road, cruised Fairmont Avenue, and sped up Gilmer Road. We only stopped to get something to eat from McDonald's, then kept going. Dave was a better driver than I thought; He just missed hitting a couple of trucks, beat a train to a railroad crossing, made a bunch of turns without hitting the brakes, and made three U-turns in a span of 10 seconds. Myself, I thought it was GREAT. I hated to go home I was having so much fun. (Good thing I outgrew all this.) But all good things must come to an end, so finally, he dropped me off at the house. But there would be other trips...

My other best friend in high school was someone I had known since our days at Judson Middle School. We were more alike than people realized (including ourselves) and from the sixth grade on, we were what one would call "friendly, serious competitors." It didn't matter what the game or sport was or whether or not we were on the same team, we were out to win. We started out playing football against each other, then checkers, Chinese checkers, bingo, tic-tac-toe, basketball, hand-held electronic games (Whatever happened to those games?), and other various board games. We would try to kill one another wrestling, or race our bicycles as if we were trying to win the Indianapolis 500. Then as we got older, we moved on to dominoes, pool, arcade games, more basketball, video games, bowling, and anything else we could think of. I would try to beat his head in; he would try to totally cremate me. Somehow before we actually succeeded in destroying each other, we learned that, *Hey, we make a better team whipping on others than just on each other.* And so, a team was formed.

Ladies and gentlemen, meet my evil twin, Devin Micheals.

OK, he wasn't really evil (depending on whom you asked) and he really wasn't my twin, but he was as close as a real brother could be to me. He was one of the few who could have me crying laughing or laughing crying. His impressions of various football and basketball players (as well as coaches) were killers, as was his ability to imitate and mimic pro wrestlers. These usually had me laughing so hard I felt like I was going to pass out. Like a lot of others around our age and older, we were serious wrestling fans from the time we could kind of comprehend what was going on. We were "old school" all the way, raised and bred on *Mid-South Wrestling.*

It's also kind of funny how we became such buddies. Or, as most of our female counterparts put it, we were the "twins". Because during our ninth and tenth grade years, I hardly saw Devin. If we passed each other in the hallway or in the locker area, we'd speak, but that was very, very seldom. Devin was one of the many classmates I knew and saw a lot of at Judson, but not at LHS my first couple of years. I guess, on one hand, because of the high school being such a large place it was easy for myself and others who were naturally quiet to go unnoticed and not run into many classmates. On the other hand, at that time, I had an abundance of classes with kids who had previously either went to Foster Middle School or Forest Park Middle School, and that trend continued throughout my years in high school

During our junior year however, Devin and I started hanging together between classes and during football practice, and this continued into our senior year, where we finally had a class together for the first time since we were at Judson. The class was Economics, taught by Mr. Polawski. This class would turn out to be one of the most difficult classes in high school. At least, that's how Devin felt about it, and about a couple hundred other students felt the same way. I really didn't feel that way partly because I was taking Calculus also that year, which, to me, made Economics look like "Hooked on Phonics". Calculus <u>*was the*</u> hardest class bar none. (More on this later.) But Economics was a challenge nonetheless.

One of my favorite "Devin moments" occurred during Economics. Mr. Polawski, as he was prone to do, announced a surprise pop quiz one day. "Clear your desks and get out a sheet of paper and number your paper from one to *three*."

What? We all probably thought that at the same time. I wasn't totally caught off guard as I had already learned to be prepared for anything in this class, but a *three-question pop quiz?*? You miss one question, you basically fail the quiz! I was thinking to myself, *Holy crap. I'm in trouble*, but when I looked back at Devin and saw the look on *his* face, I thought to myself, *Correction: we're in trouble.* The poor fellow looked like he had swallowed a cat. Our grades were already borderline passing and this quiz looked like the death-blow to knock us into the land of F (Which is for Failing). Not only that, this was the first year of the dreaded "No Pass, No Play" rule which forbid high school athletes to participate in sports or any other extracurricular activities if they were failing any classes. Even though this was the state of Texas, and high-school football was like a god here, there were some people who hated football and sports period (God forbid!) and these people came up with rules and laws like this to "put the emphasis on where it belonged-our education." Since football was more important in our young minds than anything else at the time, we *had* to pass. I was trying not to laugh when I looked at Devin because Devin looked so stricken it was as though he had spoken with the Grim Reaper himself. It was tough not to laugh. However after Mr. Polawski asked the first pop quiz question, he looked at Devin and said, "Devin, you all right back there? You're looking like Casper the Friendly Ghost back there." The whole class laughed and I had to also, because when I looked at Devin, he really did look as white as a clean sheet back there. (Sorry, brother.) But just like with the Marc Antony speech, there was a happy ending as we both (somehow) passed the pop quiz. I still called Devin

"Casper" or "ghost" for a couple of weeks afterwards though.

Devin would get me back, however. Our Economics class had a lot of girls in it, and sometimes we got "side-tracked" from what we were supposed to be doing (learning Economics) by paying attention to what they were doing (trying to get our attention and succeeding). And in Mr. Polawski's class, that's a no-no. This was a dangerous thing because he would high-side (old-school term for *ranking*) you in a millisecond if he caught you not doing what you were supposed to be doing (work), or doing what you're not supposed to be doing (talking, sleeping, acting up). At times, that could be worse than a write-up and a trip to the principal's office.

Sadly Devin got me one time when I was lacking good sense. For some reason, I had taken it upon myself to help the poor, fragile, female souls of the class with their work. Being the gentleman I was, I left my desk to go help my friend and soon-to-be girlfriend, Annette, when she called me to come over to her desk and help her. Not only was I helping her, but I was also helping Wendy, Joyce, and a few other "lost" feminine souls. Mr. Polawski had left the room, supposedly to go use the restroom, so I figured I had time before he got back. But being the dummy I was at that moment, I was wrong. He came back quicker than I thought and caught me at Annette's desk. "HEY!! WHAT THE HELL DO YOU THINK YOU'RE DOING?" he bellowed. I nearly jumped out of my skin! He was like a bad explosion–"Get back to your desk! You must think you're some kind of Don Juan or something! Go sit down!" As the class roared with laughter, I slinked back to my desk. I looked at Devin who laughed as if this was the funniest thing he had ever seen in his entire life, and I thought to myself, *He got me. I'm dead.* And at that moment, I was wishing I was. Devin didn't let me forget that for a *looong* time. "Look out! It's Don Juan! Hide the women!" he would yell at various times during our senior year, and girls would take off running, screaming, and laughing.

"Ha Ha, very funny, Devin," I told him once, wishing the ground would swallow me up in one big gulp. But isn't that was what best friends were for, anyway? To revel in our embarrassing moments?

CHAPTER 2

September to Remember

Monday, September 2, 1985

My main concern as far as the beginning of school went was that I did not want to have to ride the bus for the fourth straight year. Seven straight years if one counted middle-school-I could drive, but not too well, and I didn't have my drivers' license anyway. My parents had tried to teach me how to drive three years earlier, and all I had succeeded in doing was wrapping the family car around a very strong tree. That ended that lesson quick. It also ended any chance I had in getting my drivers' license in a decent amount of time. So I figured that maybe I could catch a ride with Dave to school and that way I wouldn't have to ride the bus. Unfortunately, I hadn't heard from him since he went out of town a couple weeks prior, and it was beginning to look like he was going to miss the first day of school anyhow since he obviously hadn't came back yet. I had always hated riding the bus for all kinds of reasons dating back to my days at Judson. The kids riding the bus were usually mean, the bus drivers were usually stupid, and the buses were usually very nasty inside. Also, it never seemed to come on time going to and leaving school. That's a lot of negatives. The only positive I could gather from all this was at least I wouldn't have to ride it in the evening time because of football practice.

This was also to be Flower-child's first year in high school, and the first time we'd be attending school together since we were at Jodie McClure. She was nervous, but not too nervous because her big brother was going to be there with her. Which, for her, was good, because I could still remember my very first day of high school and how scared I was to be going to such a big school *by myself*. I didn't have no big brothers or sisters to follow like say Devin did when we entered high school (he had two older sisters), meaning I was basically on my own as far as support and everything else went. (And I made a mess of that first day by going to the wrong class <u>twice</u> and the wrong lunch period, all before the day was halfway over with! What a nightmare.) Flower and I got along pretty good usually; I was not the mean big brother and she was not the annoying little sister. Not most of the time anyway. As far as brother-sister relationships went, ours was above-average. I had told her what to expect from certain teachers I had in the past and if she needed help finding a room or something, she knew where to find me and I'd help her. (Maybe I was *too* nice for a big brother.)

She was going to have it easy this year. I hope I would, too. This would be the first time we would attend school together since 1978, the year we moved back to Longview…

Welcome Back to Longview: July, 1978

I can still remember looking out the window of my bedroom the very first day we moved into our house on Margo Street and the first thought that came into my mind was, *I miss Abilene*. I wasn't very happy about leaving my friends in Abilene, but it wasn't my choice. My daddy had retired from the Air Force, and we were going to settle down in Longview. Well, at least it wasn't Fort Worth, or God forbid, Marshall we were going to live, and as I was told later, it could have very easily been those two places instead of Longview. Thank God it wasn't or else this book would be titled something else, like "Panthers, Bulldogs, and Mavericks." Yuck. It was during this time while the furniture was being moved into the house that we met our next door neighbors. A little boy who looked to be Poinsettia's age came over to see what was going on. We talked to him for a little while and we asked him what his name was. He said, "My name is Thomas." And he, his sister, and his family had moved next door only a month before we did. So basically, we all had moved to our new homes just about at the same time. We told him our names, and a few minutes later, his sister, Charlotte, came and joined us. She was a nice-looking girl, about the same skin-color as myself, had medium-length hair, and was a little taller than I was. We all got acquainted and became friends. I was happy about making new friends so quickly because I had gotten used to having a good friend next door to play with (as I had with Robert in Abilene), and we were all around the same age. Flower and Thomas were the same age, 6 years-old at the time, I was 9 years-old, and Charlotte was 10 going on 11 years-old.

It's funny how when one looks back at the past, one thinks, *Man, how corny can we get?* But really, maybe those were corny times, but they were also fun, innocent, and unforgettable times. We played a lot of games together back then: Frisbee, kickball, football, hide-and-seek, dodgeball, red rover, and other games kids don't play with one another anymore. One of the first games Thomas, Charlotte, Flower and I played together was the now-extinct game of jacks. It was a game where you take a small rubber ball, bounce or throw it up in the air, and you grab as many jacks (they were metal, star-shaped-looking things) as you can or as many as you're supposed to grab. Usually we played on our porch or in the driveway or in our kitchen on the floor, and we made this game as competitive as we could. It may seem boring today, but back then, the game was actually fun.

One time when the game _really_ could've gotten fun occurred when Charlotte and I were playing jacks on the porch by ourselves. I was only 9, but Charlotte was wearing some very short shorts that hot, summer day and she was sitting Indian-style, and I was like very interested in her shorts. So much so that I kept staring at them and not paying attention to the life and death struggle of a game of jacks. She was really beating me pretty good and I was too distracted to play with some jacks as puberty was starting to kick in a little early. Anyway, either she was watching my eyes or reading my mind (or possibly thought the game needed some more excitement), because she then asked me (or suggested) if we could go into the woods and have some real fun. (What kind of fun? You know.) There were plenty of woods behind our houses where you could hide a truck or two much less two horny little kids, and I seriously thought about it for a minute or two. But my sanity quickly returned when I heard my momma's voice call from inside the house asking us what we were doing. (No, she didn't hear us trying to make plans at an early age.) I replied, "Playing jacks." Then I, very courteous, very nicely and very stupidly turned Charlotte down, and we resumed our not-so-fun-anymore game of jacks.

Another time, the four of us were playing another fun game, the game of throwing a Frisbee back and forth. (Isn't it incredible how these exciting games seem to fade away over time?) We were taking turns throwing a Frisbee to one another, running and chasing it, catching it, and so forth and so on. Anyhow, we were doing all this in our front yard, where most all of our neighborhood fun would take place in the next three or four years, and it must've felt like we were playing on a football field like Texas Stadium because after awhile, one of us had the notion to throw the Frisbee high and long,...and onto the top of the roof. (It must have been Thomas who threw it.) Well, game over.

None of our dads were at home right then; they was at work. Momma was in the house and she sure wasn't going to go and climb upon the roof to get a Frisbee. I knew this because in Abilene one bright spring day, I had the superb idea of making my Superman action figure fly in the air until I threw it, totally out-of-control, onto the top of our roof. Needless to say, with Daddy being overseas at the time, Superman sat on top of the roof for a good year and a half until we had one of those nice windy rainstorms, then he got blown off the roof back into the yard a little wet, but no worse for the wear. The point was: Momma did not try to get the thing off the roof back then no matter how much I cried, whined, and sulked (which I wasn't going to do too much if I wanted to continue living), and now at this point in time, she was not going to do it now. "Well," I said, "I guess that's it. Let's go play jacks!" (No, I didn't say that back then.) But I did think the game was over and that we had to think of something else to do until Daddy got home. However, I was in the minority. "We could stand on each other's shoulders until someone could reach the roof, climb up, and get the Frisbee!" I recall Thomas saying, "Or we could stack chairs until they reach the roof, climb the chairs, get onto the roof and get the Frisbee!" Flower-child hollered, not yet mature enough to even stack pancakes. "Or Flower could stand on my shoulders or your shoulders, Cedric, and get the Frisbee," said Charlotte. Thinking these kids had all lost their minds, I told them all of their ideas were not good ideas and that we should just forget it and get on with the jack playing. Besides Charlotte was wearing those short shorts again and I was interested in them again. (I'm kidding, really.) I thought we should just leave the Frisbee on the roof and find something else to do. But I was outvoted by the inmates, and they decided with all of their wisdom to combine a couple of their ideas by stacking chairs and standing on each other until the shortest dummy, er…I mean kid, being Flower-child, could reach the roof and get the Frisbee. Me? I just stood and watched. Everything was going well, until as soon as Flower reached the roof and took hold of the Frisbee, everything and everybody came a-tumbling down. Chairs, Thomas, Charlotte, and finally, Flower-child came crashing down to Earth, the latter landing squarely on her head. It must've been either the noise of the car crash, er…I mean chair crash, or the screaming of Flower-child in pain from her near-concussion that brought Momma running outside.

After finding out what had happened and after literally dragging Flower and I into the house, she proceeded to give *ME* a whipping. And incredibly, I got so much of a whipping it was as if I had pulled the chairs away and made them all fall on purpose. (Sometimes, considering how I was punished, I wished I *had.*) Momma had put it all in perspective when she said that as I was screaming as I was getting whipped that I didn't do anything, she had replied at the time, "You're right. You didn't do *ANYTHING!*" And she kept on beating my behind until I felt just as bad as my sister did. I did not understand it back then, and you talk about being an angry little boy; I was angry enough to challenge the devil to a fight; but as I grew older, I understood the why of it all, but just barely.

Tuesday, September 3

It was the first day of school and I was back at Longview High School again, riding the stupid bus to school to begin my final year. Actually, it wasn't too bad. Nobody gave anybody else any hassles and it was pretty quiet. My classes weren't too bad, either, classmate-wise and teacher-wise. First period I had Economics with Mrs. Jolly as my teacher. (No, she wasn't a *jolly* person, but she was nice.) With me in this class were A. J. Jenkins, Billy Hammond, Rayzell Dennis, and Rena Mack. I was excited to be in this class for two reasons: Mrs. Jolly was considered to be the "easy" Economics" teacher (which I conveniently discovered after taking my first test in the class; I made a 100.), and I finally had a class with Rena, who I'd known for a long, long time since we were in the fifth grade together at Jodie McClure Elementary, and who was very fine and nice-looking. Great. I was already thinking about going with her.

Second period was my Advanced English class with Mrs. Wells as my teacher. She was also a very nice teacher, but unfortunately, I knew I wasn't going to be in that class for much longer. More on that later. Sherry Ellis, Nina Blue, and Francine Scott were also in that class, but like myself, only temporarily so. Office Aide class, which consisted of running errands for the front office, counselors, and attendance clerks, doing some sorting and filing, and studying and doing homework for other classes was my third period class. With me in this class were Shelia Mars and (can you believe it) Rena again. Ironically, the three of us all were in Miss Stone's room back in the 5th grade.

4th period was Athletics and varsity football, and 5th period was my most difficult course: Calculus. In this class, for the first time in all of my years at LHS, I had a class with Jocelyn Jones, who may have been the smartest black female student in our senior class. I'd get a chance to watch her in action for a change and maybe learn something from her. One thing about her: Not only was she very smart, but she was super-confident. Maybe some of her confidence would rub off on me. And last but definitely not least, the most enjoyable and most fun class I've ever had at LHS was my final class, Spanish II, which I had 6th period. In this class were the memorable Curtis Vines (more on him later), David Morriston, David Bertram, Pookie Blue (Nina's little sister), Devitra Figures, Tiana Mack, and of course, Randressa "Call me "Randi", "Call me anytime" Roberts. (You'll be hearing more about this crazy class in a later chapter.) All in all, it wasn't a bad schedule. In fact, it was a **GREAT** schedule. Too bad it wouldn't last...

Wednesday, September 4

Dave came to school today after missing yesterday, and I found out that for the first time since we've been at LHS we didn't have a class together. Fortunately, that would change next semester. Over the past three years, Dave and I had discussed everything from the plight of the Dallas Cowboys to some of the weirdest teachers we'd ever seen at Longview High. We'd talked about selling comic books via mail-order and even formed a small business, which didn't last, of course. (We didn't have *that* many comic books to sale.) And we discussed, of course, what girls were worth trying to talk to. It was while considering the latter subject that Dave came up with his "Machine Gun Theory" (MGT). It was very simple, actually. A guy talks to an inordinate number of girls with the sole purpose being that one of them would wind up going with him and becoming his girlfriend in the short (not long) run. (This was *not* designed to enable a guy to have more than one girlfriend; not unless he just wanted more than one. Then he was abusing the MGT to an extent.) Dave basically developed this theory over the summer while vacationing in Dallas in order to give us both something to look forward to our senior year. I think he had already succeeded for himself *before* he put his theory to the test by going with Carlina Rodriguez. But then again, he *was* also talking to this other girl he had met over the summer. Carlina and Dave had been hanging together a lot the last few months even though they weren't going together. And if one included his seeming interest in yet this other girl who happened to live in nearby Tyler, then maybe he was still testing out his theory. Since I was already brimming with confidence (and stupidity) from my junior year, I decided to go for it myself by trying to talk to three girls at one time! I hadn't forgotten about Kelly Woodson yet (Remember that name), and of course Traci Richards was still on my mind (Remember that name also), and since I had two classes with Rena Mack, she was definitely a target also. I couldn't believe I was doing this, but oh well...

Thursday, September 5

"I'm the only boy left in my English class," I said. That could've been a good thing, but actually, it wasn't.

"The English test (to stay in Advanced English) was predictably hard. Everybody seems to have gotten out of Advanced English."

"What about Spanish? How's that going?" asked Dave.

"Spanish is boring," I replied. (But believe you me that would change DRASTICALLY!)

"And so far, nothing is going on with the MGT."

But that was temporary, also. During the summer, another "old friend" had been talking to my sister a lot, and some people thought she was doing that so she could talk to me. And though I thought about asking her, I didn't feel that Comesha Farmer was all that interested in me anyhow. We'd been friends since we were five and six years old (she was a year younger than me, therefore she was a junior) and sometimes there seemed to be an attraction there and sometimes there didn't. But I admit I thought about it...but not for long. I preferred older women anyhow.

Friday, September 6

The pep rally for our football team was a mess. This was the first year of having pep rallies in the morning beginning at 7:30 a.m. instead of, as in past years, having them at 2:30 in the afternoon where everyone was in the gym making noise, and because of that, I got there late and didn't get a chance to be introduced. Oh well, at least I *did* get to walk out with the varsity football team last year a couple of times at pep rallies even though I was on the J.V. team. And believe you me, I felt I had *finally* arrived when that happened. I wasn't the only one who was late, and invariably, the whole thing sucked. I never went to another morning pep rally, until the Homecoming one and the two or three we had after that one. Not too surprisingly during our game against Fort Worth Eastern Hills that evening, it poured rain the whole time. But fortunately, we won, 17-0. During the game, I thought about the very FIRST time I played football and fell in love with the sport...

Football is King: September 1978

In the fall of 1978, Flower-child and I got ready to attend elementary school, which was for myself, yet another school. I was nine years old going on ten, but this would be my *fourth school* I'd be attending. Needless to say, I was about as excited as someone on the way to yet another funeral. The school we would be attending was right down the street from our house (only a block). In fact, I could see it from my bedroom window. The school's name was Jodie McClure Elementary. Deep down, I wanted to go back to East Ward, the school I attended in the first and second grades when we lived in Longview before, but I knew I couldn't. I was going to be in the fifth grade, so actually I'd be going to this school only one year before going on to middle school. Again, I was very excited about that bit of information also. (Sarcasm) Anyway I remember joking with Flower-child on the morning of the first day of school that she'd probably get some mean, fat, scary teacher and hopefully I'd get a nice, pretty, young teacher. Something I hadn't had since the first grade. All I had was old, mostly mean, and boring teachers. I guess I was a clairvoyant; Flower got exactly what I had predicted she get-an old, big and scary teacher. Plus, she was black (Flower's first), and black teachers didn't play back then. I truly felt sorry for Flower as Momma and I left her in her classroom and went on to my classroom. My teacher happened to be exactly what I had hoped I would get: a young, pretty, and nice teacher named Miss Stone. Seeing her helped alleviate some of my stress about being the "new kid" in a new school again, but seeing my classmates interact with each other made me definitely feel like the "new kid" once again. Fortunately, I wasn't the only new kid in the room, or even new person in the room. This was my teacher's first year teaching, so she was also new to the school and her students. I was sitting next to this boy named Doug who also happened to be a new student like myself. So, my first few days of school were spent talking to him mostly.

I was worried about whether or not I was going to make a good impression on my teacher and my classmates, and I was kind of concerned about going from basically an all-white school environment to a basically mostly-black school environment. But in reality, I didn't need to worry. Unlike Flower, whom I felt most of her angst was due to her age at the time, and who reacted miserably in the beginning to going to a different school with different kids (She was having nightmares and crying and whining that she wasn't going back to "that school", and she was very afraid of her teacher), I, on the other hand, made friends quickly and easily, and became very popular with everyone. I thought, *Wow, how did that happen*? I thought about this due to the fact that I was a shy and quiet person, most of the time. I figured it was because since I was being the nice guy I was during the first couple of months of the school year, I was willing to help my classmates with their work and help them do well because that was what I wanted to do. (No, I wasn't bribed or bullied.) My 5th grade classmates at the time (such as Tangie Alston, Marvin Bertram, Ron Lane, Robert Tabor, Rena Mack, Shelton Murphy, Dana

Tolliver, LaSandra Reese, Shelia Mars, Charles Temple, Christopher Everett, Doug Cole, Kim Harrison, and Tony Royal) really appreciated my help and we all became good friends that way. Another thing I liked to do at the time was draw. I drew pictures of super-heroes, made comic strips, and later drew pictures of sports figures. I'd give some of these pictures to my friends who liked how I drew and wanted the pictures to stick in their binders. Plus, I almost always brought a lunch to school, and normally I'd share with some my classmates. That's the key word: sharing. I was almost always willing to share with my friends and classmates and they accepted me very quickly.

How quickly? When it came time to vote on who was going to be our classroom president which was done around the third week in school in September, I and this girl named Kelcie Heron were nominated. The winner would be president of our class, the loser would be vice-president. I lost by one vote, 11-10, so I became vice-president. Actually, if I had voted for myself, I would have won. But I felt Kelly deserved to be president so it didn't bother me at all to lose. (My friends, however, thought differently.) I guess I had a quiet charisma about me back then, I don't know. Two notes: Kelly moved away within a couple of weeks after winning the election, so I did become the class president. Who became vice-president? I'm pretty sure if my memory serves me correctly it was Rena, considering how some things turned out later. She was a *great* vice-president. (Smile)

In the fall of 1978, something else happened that would change my life forever.

I became interested in...FOOTBALL!!

History lesson: The first football game I ever just sat and watched was Super Bowl X between the Dallas Cowboys and Pittsburgh Steelers in 1976. At the time, I was seven years old and I had no idea what I was watching. My daddy, if he happened to be home, every now and then would watch a football game, but he wasn't no great fan of the sport back then. Neither was I. When the Super Bowl was on, we'd watch it (I recall watching the 1977 and 1978 Super Bowls), but again, I had no idea what I was watching nor did I care very much.

While we were living in Abilene, a friend of mine gave me some football cards he didn't want anymore, and I started slowly leaning towards learning more about the sport. Then my daddy had an auntie, Aunt Thelma, who was a huge Dallas Cowboys fan. When we would go to visit her, she was always watching the Cowboys play on TV and reacting like any diehard fan when they win or when they lose. She had Dallas Cowboys team posters, pennants, magazines, shirts, everything. One day, she asked me if I wanted one of her posters and two of her magazines, and I said, sure. Thus the seeds for my infatuation with football and the Dallas Cowboys were planted. She started giving me magazines, programs, and posters that had to do with the Cowboys (I WISH I had kept all that stuff!), and at first, I had no idea what I was reading or looking at. Another note: Football obviously was not very popular in Abilene back then possibly due to the fact of there being a town not too far from Abilene called Odessa, which had a fairly decent high school football team by the name of Permian that used to beat everybody and everything around them. So my belief was that as far as football was concerned then and even later on, there wasn't much to talk about or even to get excited about in

Abilene.

Then we moved to Longview and I started going to Jodie McClure. Back then, every boy dreamed about someday wearing the green and white of the Longview Lobos. And football, not baseball or soccer or jacks, was king. (Yes, I had to learn that.) If my class and the other fifth-grade classroom (Mr. Taylor's class) had a choice of what we wanted to play during P.E., it usually was football. The boys would play football and the girls would play kickball. Plus, Jodie McClure had a youth-league football team which consisted of 5th and 6th graders and who participated against other Longview elementary schools. So before you could be a Lobo, you could be a Bear, a Pirate, a Dragon, or a Mustang. The Jodie McClure Mustangs. Football was king, and all the boys wanted to play football. Well, almost all the boys. I still really wasn't interested in football nor did I know how to play. At this time in my life, the only sports I could play OK were kickball (not great), dodge-ball (not bad), and maybe soccer (average). Basketball was a joke as far as my having skills for that sport was concerned (In other words, I was pathetic), and I hated baseball and softball because I simply could not hit or catch. To put it mildly, I was short and un-athletic. So the first time my class went outside to play Mr. Taylor's class in a football game, I had absolutely no idea what I was doing. What I remember about that game is four things: One, my classmates whom I didn't know yet were telling me and Doug who to block and we really didn't understand the concept of blocking and probably wound up blocking each other; Two, I continuously went out for passes and no one covered me or threw me the ball (thank God); Three, Daniel Poole who was in Mr. Taylor's class, but who was put on our team because his team didn't want him (I guess they thought he was slow and fat), scored our team's only touchdown on a pass he caught and in which he *outran* everyone else; Four, we lost. After that, I was beginning to *dislike* football even more. But the second time we played against each other--everything changed for me.

The game started and proceeded as it did the last time: I was running around lost, no one usually around me. Then as we were possibly on our way to losing again, our quarterback, who was Robert Tabor this day, needed a play to help us do something, anything positive. Then Ron, who didn't know my name at the time, pointed at me and said, "How about throwing it to him? Every time he goes out there's no one covering him." I'm saying to myself, *"NO! Don't throw it to me! I don't know what I'm doing!"* But Robert said, "OK," and we broke the huddle and I'm thinking, *"Please don't throw it to me because I'll drop it and look like a fool. I hope somebody covers me for once."* But again, I ran out and there is absolutely no one around me for miles. The closest person is in Hallsville or even Abilene. I'm thinking, *"Don't throw it,"* but Robert, like an Elway, or at that time, a Staubach, looked one way then turned and looked my way and let fly a pretty pass towards me. *"Oh no!"* I'm thinking. The pass looked good then it looked like it was going to go over my head. Like a miniature Lynn Swann, I dove for the ball, caught it, juggled it, and then finally caught it. My teammates went crazy about the catch as if I had won the Super Bowl with it. I didn't score a touchdown; I was really too much in shock to get up and run, but it was a long pass and we had gotten close. I thought to myself as my teammates slapped me silly in the head, on my hands and back, *"Hey, this is COOL."* Then on the very next play, I slid on my knees and caught a low pass for a touchdown. Again, pandemonium! The new kid scored! The new kid scored! What's his name? Ceggett? Cebret? Cedric! Alright, way to go, Cegret!

From then on, I **LOVED** football. I became a Mustang, and I went from being short and clumsy and pitiful in sports to one who got to pretty decent not only in football, but in basketball and baseball, too. I was definitely a late-bloomer. I became the one who made the incredible, impossible catches whenever we played. In reality, we're talking about 5th grade football here, and the biggest games there were back then were when we would play South Ward or Bramlette or Mozelle in front of maybe a hundred people. And actually, all we did was run the ball probably 99% of the time-every blue moon we would throw a pass and half the time actually complete it. But at least I could catch and I did score one touchdown, albeit in practice, and that helped me become even more popular with my classmates

Friday, September 13

Well, I failed the English test, which meant that I would have to get my schedule changed from Advanced English to Regular English. The English test was over the summer reading we were required to do the previous summer. Since I had only read one novel and half of one out of the four novels we were supposed to have read, I made the grade I deserved. (I lost interest in reading over the summer.) Only one problem: There wasn't a 2nd period Regular English class, which meant I would have to readjust (in other words, ruin) my beautiful schedule. I couldn't touch 4th, 5th, and 6th periods, thank God, but I had to change my 1st,

2nd, and 3rd period classes around. Can you say "Goodbye, easy Economics class" and "Goodbye, Rena Mack?"

Tuesday, I saw and spoke to Traci for the first time this year. Don't ask me why it took so long for me to talk to her. She was one of those intimidating, "too-good-and-too-fine-for-ya" pretty black girls. Our conversation probably went something like this:

Cedric: Hi.

Traci: Hello.

Cedric: How are you doing?

Traci: Fine.

Cedric: Well, OK. Gotta go. Nice seeing you.

Traci: Bye.

As ya'll can obviously tell, I knew what I was doing when it came to girls.

Wednesday, my schedule got changed to my having Office Aide 2nd period (instead of third period) and English 3rd period, instead of second period. But again, that was not going to last because there seemed to be 100 students in that English class and something was going to have to be done about that. I was in there with Tank Thomas, our All-State linebacker, and he had me laughing the short period of time I was in that class. Also in that class was Traci, who was looking good as usual. Speaking of Traci, at this time, I thought she was going with Freddie Woods, so I took her off the MGT list. I also found out Rena was already going with someone else, so I stopped (or at least stopped thinking about) "firing" at her, too. That left only Kelly.

And speaking of old classmates, there would be tragedy on Friday (the 13th) as William Connor, another one of my classmates from Jodie McClure, passed away in a motorcycle accident that evening.

My main memory of William was one that when I think about it today, I smile, because of who we were as kids. But back then, on a rainy day in November of 1978 on a puddle-filled field outside of Jodie McClure, I definitely *wasn't* smiling.

Here's Mud in Your Eye: November, 1978

A bunch of us had decided we wanted to play football out in the rain, and incredibly, our coach, usually mean and uncaring, let us. Previously, my momma, tired of washing nasty clothes I had messed up playing football and tired of sewing torn pants and shirts, told me that if I got dirty like that again or tore one more pair of pants, she was going give me the whipping of my life. (As if she hadn't already.) So, when we went outside, that threat was definitely on my mind, if only for a little while. I loved football, so there I went.

I was going to play no matter what, but I was going to try to be very careful. Very careful--trust me. (*Good luck on that, kiddo*, someone should've told me.) Anyway, we were supposed to be playing touch football, not tackle, due to the weather, so I wasn't too worried about getting dirty. After a while, though, I should've been. As I recall, one of my classmates threw me a pass, which I caught, and I turned to run upfield. William was on the other team and he and some of his teammates quickly cut me off. I started to cut back and as I did, instead of tagging me, he *pushed* me and I slid and fell into possibly the biggest puddle south of Lake O' The Pines! I looked like a pig in slop. William nearly fainted from laughing so hard. Myself, I wanted to cuss him out. I chunked the ball at him, aiming for his head, but obviously I wasn't the second coming of Roger Staubach, so I missed. I think I did call him one or two bad names before I ran into the school. I took off my clothes in the bathroom and tried to wash them out in the sink. I could <u>not</u> go home like that or I'd be counting welts. Needless to say, I walked around school the rest of that day, soaking wet, but clean. And I went home that way and ran into the house and changed clothes before my mom saw me. Thanks, William, for almost getting me into trouble.

Friday, September 20

Not very much would happen this week. My schedule was still in the process of being altered, and I became the new holder on kicks during football practice after our original holder and third-string quarterback quit. (Which maybe, after Friday's game, a 3-0 loss to Abilene in which we missed three or four field goals, I probably should've been doing it *during* the game.) And I finally got my class ring towards the end of the week. Next question: *Who was going to be wearing it?*

Friday, September 27

My schedule was changed for the duration of the semester. Finally. The good news: I received Office Aide 1st period, which sadly took the place of my Economics class in which I had a 100 average (NO!). If it were any consolation, I would have this class with fellow classmates Micheal London, Ben Stevens, Ronnie Dennis, and Mr. Stud himself, Curtis Vines. I had Regular English 2nd period with Mrs. Wells for my teacher again, who I really liked. The powers-that-be created this English class since previously there had not been a regular English class available that period, and obviously I wasn't the only one who didn't do much reading over the summer. Over half the original second period advanced English class had failed the test, hence the need for another regular class.

Now for the bad news: I received the hardest teacher (in a lot of my classmates' minds and mine also, at first) in the school for Economics 3rd period. His name, as mentioned earlier, was Mr. Polawski. I had heard that *over* half of his students had failed his first test and I thought, *Oh my God, and I'm going to be in his class.* I would go through this class with Wendy Bronson, Joyce Melrose, Annette Ray, and of course, the man himself, Devin M. (Otherwise known as the "Ghost".) My first day in that class, when I entered the room, everyone was looking pitiful and morose. Except Devin, who looked glad to see me. I wish I could have looked the same, but I'll admit, I *was concerned* and I looked it. I went and sat next to Devin, who told me something to calm my fears:

"Welcome to Hell, Brother."

"Thanks Devin."

Anyway, I had a 100 average (for real) in my original Economics class and I did not want to lose that. Incredibly, Mr. Polawski, in an unheard-of fit of kindness, let me keep my grades from my previous class and I was temporarily sedated.

I had also started talking to Kelly again (and not really getting anywhere). Our story had been a long one (Be patient; all of this will be covered), and for a while it seemed I had competition in one Brandon Raymond, someone I met back in the 10th grade and who was a friend of mine. But lo and behold, that Thursday, Brandon came up to me and told me he was Kelly's cousin and that I should try and go with her. He told me that he felt that she kind of liked me, but just didn't show it towards me. The way he talked, she had kinda hinted it around others that she liked me more than she let on. And I had heard this before in the past from others myself. I was already feeling great before he told me all this because Traci, out of the blue, had come up and spoken to me earlier in the day, and that in itself was an accomplishment. There will be more on Kelly *and* Traci in later chapters. Trust me on this.

Saturday, September 28: HAPPY BIRTHDAY TO ME!

I didn't do much on my birthday (17 years old, believe it or not). I went to Shreveport and got taken out to eat pizza, but other than that, it was a pretty boring day. The same, however, couldn't be said for the first month of school. It had been a highly interesting month and as the saying goes, the best (and worst) was yet to come.

CHAPTER 3

Back in the Day

Tuesday, October 3, 1985

It was unofficially "Reminisce Day" during my Office-aide 1st period class. I have had Office-aide class three different periods already during the school year. The first couple of weeks I had it third period, and then I had it second period for one day. Now for the rest of the first semester, I will have had it first period. Working my way down, I suppose that was what I was doing. What my fellow office-aiders and I mainly did was run errands for the secretary, counselors, and principals, and pick up rolls for the attendance office. So I guess you could say we were "gophers." As in, "Go for so-and-so and get this." Or, how about "go-gets?" As in, "Go get this person so we can paddle him, talk to him about his grades, his conduct, his dog and cat, and whatever else we can think of." All in all, we had fun doing those things (especially picking up rolls) and when we weren't busy, we usually were studying, doing homework, or having intelligent discussions, if you could call it that. I guess that they were intelligent enough for us. Considering that I had these classes with Micheal (who opened my mind to a lot of things), Curtis (a combination of cool and humorous), Blaine Pearson (very funny), Ben (another cool dude), and the Dennis Twins, Rayzell and Ronnie, I suppose it was a miracle I made it through my final year *period.* With friends like them, I literally laughed my way out of school. Was this Longview High School or *Saturday Night Live?* Our discussions this day would center on the incredible and stupid things that had happened in the past, and the memories started flowing.

Ronnie Dennis usually was a very serious person. He was serious about his work, he was serious about track, he was serious about girls, and he definitely was serious about pizza.

Huh?

"Do you remember that time Ronnie went crazy in Homemaking?" asked Ben.

"How could I forget since I was kind of involved in the situation back then?" I said.

"Why do you always bring that up?" asked Ronnie, looking somewhat irritated and embarrassed at the same time.

"Because, man, that was a *trip*! I couldn't believe you got mad over some pizza," Ben laughed at the memory.

"Well, I had a right to get mad! You were there. You saw what happened. Heck, Cedric was in my group. He knows that that teacher was wrong! You remember what happened, don't you?" Ronnie asked me.

"Yeah, I remember," I said…

The Big Pizza Argument: Friday, March 25, 1983

The sad (and yet, funny) story took place three years ago back when we were in the ninth grade. I was taking Homemaking--the cooking part of the course--and Mrs. Oster was our teacher. She divided the class into five groups of four, and basically, to get a good grade, each group had to cook whatever was required each week. One time, it was pancakes; another time it was hamburgers. And one interesting day, it was pizza. My group consisted of myself, Johnny Cross, Charlie Fisher, and Ronnie. We were the only group to consist of all boys; all the other groups had at least one girl in the group who could cook, so we were already at a disadvantage due to the fact that at the time, none of us in our group could cook, much less fix a bowl of cereal. We burned up cookies, pancakes, waffles, and ourselves. (I tried to take a tray of cookies out of the oven *without* the oven mitt and got predictable results: burned fingers and burned cookies on the floor.) Our hamburgers weren't done, and our hot-dogs could have jumped off the tray and took off running by themselves. Each group usually got to eat whatever they prepared, but I always either gave my share to Johnny or Ronnie, or I threw it in the trash since I kind of valued my health. I figured we were on the way to a terrible grade until the day we made pizza.

In a way, I was looking forward to fixing a pizza since that was one of the (very) few things I knew how to cook (thanks to Daddy). And so with the group following my lead, our pizza came out very good. We had finally made something eatable. Ironically, even though I helped cook the pizza and actually did most of the work, I still didn't want to eat any of it (health issues), and so I gave my share to the rest of the group. Charlie didn't want too much of it either, so Johnny and Ronnie had the two biggest slices. Somehow, we had divided up the pizza before Mrs. Oster could get her sample slice (for a grade), so she decided she would take some of Ronnie's pizza for her sample. At first, Ronnie mildly protested. However, after cutting her slice off of his slice, and taking the biggest portion of the two, which it looked like for all the world she was taking seven-eighths of it and leaving him an eighth of the slice, Ronnie went off. Which, incidentally, reminded me of the *Tom and Jerry* cartoon where the cat (Not Tom; I think the other cat's name was Butch) cut off a very small piece of the turkey that was on the table, but instead of taking the small piece he cut, he took the <u>whole</u> turkey! At first, it was funny because I (and probably the rest of the class) didn't think Ronnie was *that* serious over a slice of pizza. Plus, I thought Mrs. Oster was playing at first because it *was* such an unnecessary large slice she kept. I thought she was going to say something like, "I'm just playing with you, Ronnie. Give me the smaller slice." But I was wrong. When she saw Ronnie's reaction, she kept the larger slice. And to put it kind of mildly:

Ronnie was P.O.'d.

Very P.O.'d.

He refused to let Mrs. Oster have that slice of pizza. In fact, she had to *take it* from him. (<u>*That*</u> was funny.) Lost in all this was the fact that Johnny's slice was the same size, if not bigger, as Ronnie's original slice. If anything, I'm pretty sure Ronnie was thinking that Mrs. Oster should have taken some of Johnny's slice instead of his. But she didn't, and he exploded like an atomic bomb. He got so mad that he ran out of the class and told Mrs. Oster to go to hell. For real. And soon. Next thing we knew, the principals and various other school personnel were chasing him outside all through the tennis courts. I observed all this and shook my head while some of us laughed as if it was the funniest thing they'd seen since Bozo the Clown.

Ronnie never came back to class. Ronnie got suspended for God-knows-how-many days. Johnny ate Ronnie's pizza as well as his own.

"Incredible, ain't it?"

"I'll never forget that day as long as I live," said Ronnie.

"Neither will I."

Ronnie's brother, Rayzell, was an artist. I mean, the boy *could* draw. Being somewhat of a decent artist myself, I could appreciate any type of artwork done by him, Corey Carter, and Mark Grell, all of whom were my classmates. They were all in the Art Club and got to take part in various contests and exhibitions, and express themselves through their art. If I hadn't had an art teacher who disliked me back in the ninth grade, I would have been in that club also. For some reason, she just did not like me, and the feeling was mutual. She thought everything I drew was a piece of sh**, when in reality, I was probably the best artist in her 1st period class. I'm not bragging-that was a <u>fact</u>. Anyway, Rayzell, Corey, and Mark could draw three times better than me, meaning they could have taught the art classes themselves. Rayzell was serious about his art, more so than anyone else I knew. He always said he was going to be a graphic designer or artist someday, and he was one of the few who actually constantly worked towards that goal while in middle and high school. I never saw him without drawings or designs of some type. In fact, even though I had known Ronnie since the 9th grade, Rayzell and I didn't become good friends until we were seniors. He always had looked real serious to me, but I learned he can joke with the best of them. And he always seemed to be surrounded by the prettiest girls.

"Why don't you share some of those with me?" I'd kid him.

"You couldn't handle it," he'd reply, "you're not strong and tough enough for women like this."

"Yeah, right."

Then there was the time Micheal London tried to get me to ask Calacia Hill to be my date for the prom. Let me tell you about Calacia Hill:

Calacia Hill was probably the most beautiful girl in our senior class. And if anyone had told me eleven years earlier, back when Calacia and I were in the first grade together, that she would grow up and become not only the Homecoming Queen but be voted Most Beautiful Girl in our class four straight years, I would have said, "You're absolutely right." For even back then, in the first and second grades, I could tell that she was something special. How can a little kid tell something like that? It was easy. She was cute, smart, and very talented. She could sing, dance, play musical instruments, and say her multiplication tables quicker than even myself. And just like during our high school years together, she intimidated me in elementary school as well to a certain extent. Don't get me wrong; I talked to her a lot when we were little kids. We were always in (friendly) competition with one another as far as who could make the highest grades or act the best, or had the cleanest desk/area, etc. We attended the same church in those days and sometimes played and worked together at school. Calacia also held the distinction of being the first girl who ever called me on the phone back when we were in the second grade. She didn't say too much, and I really and truly wasn't thinking all that much about girls anyway, so I didn't appreciate the significance of that phone call back then. (If it had happened while we were in high school, I'd have probably fainted.) However, she was so cute back then it was almost scary.

Speaking of that second-grade year, I had an anxiety attack like no other that year, and it involved Calacia. Here's the story:

Let's Pretend We're Married: Spring, 1976

Our second-grade teacher was named Mrs. Morris. She was, bar none, the meanest teacher at East Ward Elementary and the meanest teacher I've ever had, period. She loved to paddle kids and would call us by our last names, not our first names, if she wanted something. It would be like, "**EDWARDS! GET OVER HERE! NOW!!**" And I'd run over to her desk, like a chicken with its neck chopped off. She was just like a drill sergeant, and if you didn't do something right, she'd let you know about it in no uncertain terms. She made a lot of us cry that year, in more ways than one. Yeah, Mrs. Morris was mean, and sometimes cruel.

One day, we happened to be studying pantomime (of all things), and instead of having us just simply reading about it and drawing pictures or something, she decided she was going to make examples out of a couple of us and make the victims act out a pantomime. She chose this boy named Scott and a girl whose name was Amber to do the pantomime. Not only that, she told them exactly what they were going to be doing. "**TUCKER! TAYLOR! YOU'LL BE DOING A PANTOMIME IN FRONT OF THE CLASS OF BEING A HUSBAND AND WIFE! GET STARTED! NOW!!**"

O-kay. There were three things wrong with this. First, this was going to be done in front of the *entire* class. The entire, *laughing* class. Second, this was 1976, not 2006 or even 1986. Little boys did not like little girls back then, and didn't want to have anything to do with little girls short of pushing them down and beating them up or something of that nature. (How things change.) We especially didn't want to do anything that had to do with love, marriage, romance, and the like. Third, Amber liked Scott. I mean, *really liked Scott*. Scott, on the other hand, was practically terrified of Amber. If it had been any other teacher that had told him to do this, he probably would have said, *No thank you*, or turned red and pretended he was sick. But this being Sgt...,uh...I mean, Mrs. Morris telling him to do this, he really had no choice. (Unless he liked getting paddled.) Of course, Amber was really into it, playing a wife to the hilt, while Scott frowned and winced through the whole thing. And, of course, it was funny, and we all laughed. Mrs. Morris told us to shut up. Usually we'd obey Mrs. Morris no matter what, but when Amber kissed Scott on the lips, and Scott looked and acted as though he had been made to drink soiled toilet water, the class erupted in laughter. Not even Mrs. Morris could stop this. While Amber pranced ultra-happily to her seat, Scott trudged over to his desk as if he were on his way to the electric chair. (He probably wished he were.) We didn't care; we all laughed our heads off, myself included. I felt like I was going to bust a gut laughing. Mrs. Morris looked at the class for a few moments, and then she looked right at me. This was like the devil himself (herself?) looking at me right before he got ready to throw his pitchfork. I had no idea what was about to happen, but I knew it was going to be BAD:

"**TOMORROW,**" Mrs. Morris boomed, "**EDWARDS AND HILL**

WILL DO THE PANTOMIME OF BEING MARRIED!"

I instantly stopped laughing.

The class had slowed its laughter while Mrs. Morris spoke, but after her announcement, the class shook with more laughter, with me looking like I had peed on myself. My head started spinning with the anticipation of more humiliation. I did not even look at Calacia; if I had and she had smiled at me or something, there's no telling what I would've done. Cry, scream, sweat, throw up, take your pick. I imagined myself going through what Scott had just gone through, and the more I thought about it, the sicker I felt. Needless to say, I was no good the rest of the day, evening, and night. I didn't eat supper, play with any of my toys, and of course, I couldn't sleep. Momma asked me what was wrong, but I couldn't and didn't tell her. If I had, it would not have done any good. She would've told me, "Too bad. You're still going to school tomorrow. Be tough!" (To paraphrase a popular song, *Parents just don't understand*.) Flower-child was too little to understand at the time, and she would not have cared either. No, I was doomed and I knew it. I was going to be the "sacrificial Scott" tomorrow. That night, I prayed and asked God to let Mrs. Morris forget the whole thing...

The following day, I sweated and sat quietly at my desk through math time, milk break, reading time, puppet time, and lunch time until it was English (and pantomime) time. Again, I didn't look at Calacia. I did not want her thinking I wanted to do this. In fact, I don't think she wanted to do this either, for she didn't say anything about it. Amber would've brought it up instantly. But Calacia sat right behind me, quietly looking at her English book. Mrs. Morris started going over the English lesson.

Pantomiming wasn't mentioned at all. (Whew!! And I guess that's why people either have a fear of or a dislike of mimes, because of bad experiences like this one I have just described from my childhood. By the way, I had always wondered whether or not Calacia even remembered that day, and yes, later on, I did ask her. Fortunately, she didn't remember anything about pantomiming so she probably purged it from her memory.) Anyhow, I had been saved from having to kiss Calacia! Thank you, God. (I think)

My friends laughed at the story about Calacia and me, and then Micheal asked me something very interesting:

"Why don't you go up to Calacia and ask her to go to the prom with you?"

I thought that Micheal was tripping, as usual. Me? Ask Calacia to be my date for the prom? Did I want to die? No way, and that's what I told Micheal. "I don't feel like making a fool out of myself today. Besides, there is *no* way she'd want to go with me, and anyway, she probably already has a date for the prom." It's not that I *didn't* want to ask her; I'd *kill* to be her date for the prom. But I was that...I hate to say this considering...*afraid* to ask her. She was so pretty, so beautiful, she would make me look like the bottom of the barrel just standing next to her. But for some reason, Micheal was not too convinced.

"But what if she doesn't?"

I thought about it for a moment, *"I think she already has a date. I'm sure of it. But if she doesn't, why don't you go ask her?"*

Micheal also started thinking, *"I don't know. She kind of intimidates me. She's up here, and I'm down there. I think you should ask her."*

I said, "Brother, she intimidates me, too. And my luck with girls hasn't been exactly all that great. Really, you know her better than me. You should go ask."

Micheal thought about it again, and then he said, "OK, but you come with me." I said, "OK" and walked with him towards certain doom.

Micheal and I had some real deep conversations about school and girls in particular. He was one of the few who could make me laugh and *think* about things at the same time. And strangely, we always seemed to try to give *each other* confidence, as far as girls and our schoolwork were concerned. He succeeded a lot more than I did as far as girls were concerned during our senior year, but he was a true friend in every sense of the word as he always tried to lift my spirits when I felt down. "Don't give up," he'd say, "I've got confidence in you."

When Kelly broke up with me the first time, he was the first person who tried to lift my spirits back up and not let me be so down. He basically gave me a "hit 'em again" kind of pep talk, and it helped. A friend like that you're willing to do things for. I'd try to cover for him whenever he got to school late (when we had office-aide first period) and he appreciated that. Also, when he was unsure about talking to this girl he had met in Dallas, questioning whether or not he was worthy of her, I told and convinced him that he should talk to her and that he was worthy of her. And it turned out to be very fruitful for him. He used to tell me about her every day and even showed me some pictures she had sent him. (Yes, she was hot-but I didn't tell him that; he already knew it.) They seemed to make a great couple, and I was happy for him.

Now, he had been trying to convince me to ask the prettiest girl in the school to be my prom date, and I just couldn't do it. I didn't have nowhere near enough confidence. This was the same girl I used to hit and take off running from back in the first and second grades, and back then even you could tell she was going to grow up and break boys' hearts. And I was supposed to ask her to be my date? I didn't think so. The thought was nice, but it just wasn't going to happen.

So Micheal decided he was going to be the sacrificial lamb, the brave one, the one with guts to ask Calacia to be his date. I followed him, expecting to console him after she would look at him as if he'd lost his mind, tell him "no," and walk away. I obviously had her confused with another stuck-up classmate named Lois Hudson, who was famous for doing things like that. Since this wasn't Lois whom Micheal was standing in front of, when Micheal asked Calacia to be his date for the prom, she said, "I'd love too."

His reaction was, shock, and then, joy. My reaction was *what*? If my jaw could've hit the ground, it would have, as I just could not believe what I had just heard. And neither could Micheal at first, and then he reacted pretty coolly. "OK," he said, "I'll see you later." Then he ran off and did flips. I thought to myself, *"What just happened here? He tried to get me to ask her out, I wouldn't do it, so he asks her out instead, she says, Yes, I'd love to, and he's happy, she's happy, and I'm...I'm...sick."* It sort of reminded me of 1976 in a weird and depressing kind of way.

Just then, Flower-child came by, looked at me and saw the look on my face, and said to me, "Blew it again, huh? You stupid dummy." Then like the commercial, she said, "You can learn a lot from a dummy." I just looked at her.

Then, to fittingly close out the day, Devin and I were standing in the locker area talking, and another traumatic memory was rehashed...

The First Time: September, 1983

"I'm standing in the stairwell on the top floor with this girl, see? It's during second lunch and you know how they never check those stairwells during second lunch. They do it first lunch, but that's it. Anyway, I'm with this girl, and she's like real, real fine, with the prettiest smile and the prettiest and biggest brown eyes you've ever seen. And anyway, she looks at me with those big, brown eyes and says, *Do you love me?* And I say, 'yeah.' Then she says, *Do you want me?* And I look at her and how fine she is, and I say, 'Heck, yeah.' I didn't curse because you know I don't believe in that, but anyhow, after I said that, she put her arms around me and pulled me real close to her, I mean, I could feel *everything*, then she took my hand and put it somewhere where it didn't belong, or where it wasn't used to being, if you know what I mean. Then I started shaking and sweating, and then I could feel the room starting to spin around, and I felt like I was having an asthma attack! I mean, I felt like I had <u>*NO*</u> oxygen! I could feel my mouth drying up, and if I had tried to talk right at that moment, nothing would have come out."

"Then what happened?"

'I almost fainted and fell over the stairwell balcony!"

"You're kidding!"

"For real, man! I mean she had to literally hold me up and keep me from falling over!"

"No way!"

"I'm sweating buckets, my face felt like Niagara Falls. And I had no feeling in my legs or anything else for that matter. I was breathing like I was totally out of air, trying to suck up oxygen."

"Then what happened?"

"I told her I needed to just sit down, just let me sit down."

"No, you didn't!'

'Yes, I did, too. It would've been embarrassing, except I was about to freak-out."

"What did she do?"

"She let me sit down, she asked me if I was alright, I said, 'yeah", even though I wasn't. We sat on the steps, talked a little bit, then she kissed me! Then she got up and left."

"Wow! Just left you, huh?"

"Yeah, and I was thankful she did because I thought I was having a heart attack or something."

And *that*, my friends, was the first time **Devin** officially touched a girl in high school.

Gotcha!

CHAPTER 4

Kelly and Me, Part I

Saturday, October 5

Today I spent the day thinking about the girl named Kelly Woodson and our history thus far. It's been up and down to say the least. It's hard to believe that a few years ago I felt I didn't stand a chance with any girl, especially my first official crush…

Tangela Stanley: September, 1979

Back when I started the 6th grade at Judson Middle School, one of the first things I became involved in was the Gifted and Talented Program, G.A.T.E. for short. I remembered the first G.A.T.E. meeting I had to attend and I met someone for the very first time who I will never, ever forget. When they called my name and about thirty other names over the speaker to report to the library after sixth period, I had no idea why or what for. I knew I wasn't in trouble because they had called mostly all the smart students' names, and being that they were just about all white kids, I didn't recognize some of the kids. Not yet, anyway, since this was around the beginning of school that year.

So, I sat in the library with all these other kids as this lady explained what G.A.T.E. was. Simply, it was like a club or group of smart kids who got to do things like learn to use computers and VCRs (which in 1979, were very new and different), and take part in different activities based on learning. I guess I got picked because I made real good grades and was taking advanced classes. I never bothered to find out. Anyway, I was sitting there bored, when someone tapped me on the shoulder from behind. It was a girl, a black and beautiful girl sitting behind me. She had long hair and a very friendly smile. She said, "I know you. My momma knows your momma." I did the same thing I would do for the next couple years as I got to know this girl; I would look at her with my heart in my throat, then quickly look away if she was looking at me, unable to speak until finally saying something stupid, "Uh...yeah." I practically forced the words out of my mouth. She smiled and turned back around. But I could not stop looking at her. I had liked and noticed a few girls before, but this was totally different. It was as if I were mesmerized. I just could not take my eyes off of her. And if she turned around, I quickly turned away and looked somewhere else, feeling myself turn red. From that time on, my life changed. No longer was I interested in just football, comic books, frogs, and trains. I was in love with a seventh-grader named...I forgot to ask who she was!

Back then, I talked to the Simms boys a lot: Mike, nicknamed "Cycle", Markus, and Will. Willie was in the same grade I was, but I was closer to Cycle, whom he and his twin brother Markus were both a year older and a grade higher than I was. We all became friends the year before thanks to their dog. Their dog, who they had named "Butch" even though she was a girl, used to come to our house all the time, and we would feed her some of our leftover scraps. My sister and I called her "Lil' Dog." Why, I don't know, it must've been Flower's idea. The Simms' brothers would come down the street to our house to get their dog, then later, they would come over to play football and later, basketball. Cycle and I were good friends and I usually sat next to him on the bus. We'd talk about all kinds of things: football, sports, TV shows, music, and girls. Actually, he would talk about girls, how good they looked (or were beginning to look), how ugly they looked, or something along those lines. Once he even tried to teach me how to feel on girls' behinds as they would walk by. In 1979, for some reason back then, the sport of adolescent boys at JMS (and probably at Foster and Forest Park as well) was to feel on as many girls' behinds as possible. I'll never forget Cycle saying: "You've got to pretend your hand is a spoon and spoon it like so." I respectfully declined. Actually, I did try to feel on Dana, of all people, but she turned around just when I was about to and gave me a look that was all 'Go ahead and make my day.' I decided not to make her day and changed my mind. Anyway, one day I happened to be sitting with Cycle on the bus, when I saw **her** (my dream girl) get on the bus! (The girl at the G.A.T.E. meeting, for those who haven't figured it out)

"Cycle, who is that?" I asked pointing towards her.

"That's Tangela," he said, "Tangela Stanley."

That name sounded familiar, but I couldn't figure it out right then and there why it did. My mind was in a whirl and again, I couldn't stop staring at her. Cycle noticed I wasn't paying too much attention to whatever girl, electronic game, or fight he was talking about, and he saw instantly what had happened. "You like her, don't you? You like Tangela Stanley! You like Tangela, you like Tangela, you like Tangela!" he had started singing. I told him to shut up and that I didn't like <u>any</u> girl. I was 11 years old, not 16 or 17. I still hated girls! Girls? Yuck! Of course, he didn't believe me. I didn't believe me either. Not the way I was looking at Tangela. He told me there was nothing wrong with liking Tangela, she was a very nice girl. Just looking at her, I already knew that.

Of course, when I got home, the first thing I did was ask Momma who was Tangela Stanley, and I told her that she said that her momma knew mine. My momma said, 'Don't you remember Mrs. Stanley who used to help teach you back in the first grade at East Ward? That's her daughter, Tangela." Suddenly, I remembered. Mrs. Stanley was a teacher's aide who used to help me with reading and learning new words when I was little. I also remembered thinking she looked nice for a teacher. I guess all the moving around caused me to forget about her. After Momma told me this bit of information, at first I was surprised, but then I didn't care. All I could think about was one person; No matter what I said to Cycle about what I didn't like, I knew exactly who I liked a lot at that moment.

After I found out who Tangela was, whenever we had a G.A.T.E. meeting, I would try to sit next to her. We were the only two black kids in the room, so it wasn't too hard. If we had a meeting, or happened to be in the G.A.T.E. room together, or went on a field trip along with the other students, I would try and sit by her. Sometimes, I succeeded, sometimes my shyness would get the best of me and I didn't. Sometimes I sat with her and didn't say a word. That was better than nothing. I was still in love. Tangela was not a mean person; she was very down-to-Earth and one of the nicest girls you'd ever meet. It didn't hurt that not only was she real pretty, but she was very, very talented. She could play the piano, sing, dance, play sports, was a cheerleader, and could do gymnastics. I would be in the school choir with her my 7th grade year, and we sat together a lot that year whenever we would travel and sing.

However, in December of my 6th grade year, a very good memory occurred: My family and I went to the Christmas parade that's held every year in downtown Longview right after Thanksgiving, and who did we run into? You guessed it: Tangela and her family. Tangela had a brother named Victor who was the same age as Flower, and being that they were both in the same grade, Flower already knew him before I met Tangela. Her mother, who remembered me of course, and father were all there. So, while the parents stood nearby talking about grown-up things, we kids stood together watching the parade. This was the first time I would stand next to a girl feeling the way I did at the time. Close enough to hold hands and I wanted to, more than anything in the world at that time, but I hadn't went that crazy yet, not with my parents *and* her parents standing nearby. But they weren't that close to us. Not even my smaller sister and her smaller brother were that close to us to be a distraction, maybe two feet away. I wasn't even paying attention to the parade. I wouldn't have cared less if the Dallas Cowboys, Pam Grier, Bigfoot, and the Joker had all walked by. I was standing next to and talking to Tangela without sounding and looking stupid for once (I wasn't wearing my glasses yet), and it almost felt like kind of a date. I didn't want the evening to end, but finally it did, and she said, "Goodbye, Cedric. See you tomorrow." I went home feeling really _good_.

I would say that Tangela never found out how much I really liked her, but she did-twice. The first time occurred on a bus ride home from school. By this time, I was in the 7th grade and going through a terrible year. It was springtime, naturally, and I was sitting with Cycle and super-torn and conflicted about Tangela. On one hand I was shy and didn't want anyone to know how much I liked Tangela, but on the other hand, I wanted to go with her something awful (in other words, be her boyfriend) and she would have to know how I felt about her. Cycle, who along with Devin, might have been one of the few who knew how much I liked Tangela back then, encouraged me to write her a note, expressing my feelings and asking her to go with me. So against my better judgment, I did. Tangela was sitting a couple of seats in front of me, but her books were on a shelf right above me, so I reached up and got one of her books and stuck the note in it. Right away, I got cold feet and thought to myself, *"You fool! What are you doing?"* So I reached back up and took the note out. Then I started thinking, *"This is your only chance to let her know how you feel without talking to her-Put the note back in the book-<u>DO IT</u>!"* So I reached up and put the note back. Then I got cold feet again, and pulled the note out. I did this three more times until I just sat there holding her book trying to decide what to do. Cycle said, "Do it!" Finally I satisfied myself by hiding the note inside her book cover instead of her book, and thinking, *"It'll be awhile before she finds that note. By then, hopefully I will be brave enough to talk to her."* I put the book back just in time; She got her books a minute later and got off at her stop.

    I was stressed for a couple of weeks. She never approached me or let me know she had found and gotten the letter, and after a while, I forgot about it. Then one day after school, we were getting on the bus, and I was sitting with Devin. A little later, Tangela got on the bus and she asked to sit with me. I let her in, and she sat in the middle. I was feeling the usual around her: nervous, tongue-tied, anxious, etc. Halfway home, I really wasn't focused on Tangela, I was aware of her, of course, but not really focused on her. She was talking to some of her friends behind us, and I really wasn't paying attention. They were talking about boys, I guess, then Tangela said, "This is my boyfriend right here. He wrote me a note and stuck it in my book and he didn't think I'd find it, but I did." I caught that part, and before I could react, she grabbed me and put her arms around me and was trying to hug and kiss me! Devin looked at me and said, "Ced! Is this true?" I was caught so off-guard, I had started stuttering and really couldn't get any words out. She answered for me and told Devin, yes, it was true, and he started laughing. Any other time, I'd feel as though I had died and went to Heaven, but I was feeling the opposite this time because it caught me by surprise and she was doing this in front of everybody. I put my head down as Tangela kept talking, and it was obvious to me that this was one big joke to her. I told her to get her arm out from around me and told her the biggest lie I ever told in my life up to that point: "I don't like you!" She got mad (actually play-mad) and pushed me out of the seat. I sat back down and she tried pushing me again but I wouldn't let her. Meanwhile, everybody in the middle of the bus was laughing. Tangela was saying some mean things now; I pretended not to hear her. I felt terrible. This was why I HATED riding the bus. When I got home and got off the bus, I went straight to my room. I didn't come out until the next day. Tangela and I didn't talk to one another again until the last week of school.

Tangela and her family moved away at the end of that school year-my 7th grade year and her 8th grade year. I rode my bicycle past her house numerous times before she moved, hoping she would come out. Once she did, but I didn't talk to her. I kept on down the street. When we had an end-of-the-year awards' ceremony at Judson, we both received awards and stood only inches from one another, but I was too shy and afraid to speak to her. Finally, after the ceremony was over, she came up and spoke to me.

"Congratulations on your award, Cedric."

I could barely speak from the size of my smile saying, "Thanks Tangela. Congratulations to you, too."

She smiled and walked away with her parents. Nearby, my daddy stood with Flower, and Flower said, "You really like that girl. Your lips are shaking." She laughed, but I didn't care. I watched Tangela as always as she got in her parents' car and they drove off.

I continued watching a few weeks later, as the moving truck arrived at her house. I watched them move with a heaviness in my heart. I liked her so much, but now, she would never truly know how much. That was the first time she found out.

There would be a second time, but that will be told in another book for another time. Back to Kelly, before I met her, I felt I had absolutely no chance with girls. My confidence had been shot due to my first couple of years in high school, but that would all change in 1984...

In the Beginning: Wednesday, April 11, 1984

I suppose when telling a tale of romance and woe, it's best to start at the beginning, so without further ado, here goes:

Back in the spring of 1984, when I was only a pitiful sophomore, I was suffering from a self-esteem crisis. I was going through the year not hardly talking to anyone except possibly my three or four best friends, and not a single one of them was a girl. In the past, I had crushes on certain girls (Tangela Stanley and Vanessa Hillsdale immediately come to mind) who I liked a helluva lot but felt I had absolutely no chance with. When one was shy and not noticeable anyhow, well, the self-esteem came crashing down. My self-esteem at this time was at an all-time low. I didn't really try to talk to anyone when I was in the ninth grade, and the tenth grade year was nearly over. There didn't seem to be any way for me to come out of my funk either.

Then one day while I was busy making a fool out of myself in P.E. class, I heard a voice calling down to me. "Cedric! Cedric, up here! Hi Cedric!" We were down in the gym playing basketball, and upstairs, where the ping-pong tables were, the P.E. girls were up there playing ping-pong and doing exercises. I looked up, and the girl calling out to me was Beverly Slade. I didn't know her too well, but we had History together 2nd period that year. Every now and then in class, she would speak to me as in, *Hi, how are you doing?* And I'd answer and go about my business. That was usually the extent of our conversations. She was a petite, cute girl, with medium length hair, light-skinned, and she had a nice smile. In other words, she wasn't bad-looking at all. Our conversations, however, usually lasted all of five to ten seconds. But that would all change after she called out to me that day during P.E.

I didn't think much of her calling to me at the time since I figured she was just being friendly as usual, but when she started speaking to memore during history class and calling out to me almost every day during P.E., I started thinking things. Like, *"This girl must really like me."* I knew I wasn't the best-looking or most interesting guy around, and I still was extremely shy, so I wondered to myself, *"If she does like me, why does she?"*

Obviously, I wasn't very confident in myself. My self-esteem was still poor. But every day, she'd speak, and we became better friends as a result. I still didn't feel she liked me so much she wanted us to be more than just friends, and at first, I didn't even consider the thought. Then one day I heard her tell one of her friends after she had spoken to me at P.E. that she thought I was cute and that I had cute legs. (Remember, this *was* during P.E., where we were all wearing shorts.)

Talk about a self-esteem boost!

For the first time since I entered high school, I had actually gotten a compliment from a girl other than, *He's ugly but he's sweet.* (Just kidding) Finally, I felt I actually had a chance with girls. Or at least with *one*. But that's all it took. I stopped looking at Beverly as just a friend; she was really a living, breathing, attractive, pretty, fine girl. Who liked (believe it or not) <u>me</u>! And I definitely liked her. Suddenly, I began to imagine us as more than just friends--I wanted to go with her. And why not? She was down-to-earth, she talked to me every day, she was nice to me, and of course, she was <u>cute</u>.

Fast Forward To: Thursday, May 17, 1984

And so it came to pass that as the springtime months of April and May rolled by, I began to slowly gather the courage to ask Beverly to be my girlfriend. Finally, towards the end of school, after much debating, I wrote her a note. (Interestingly, this was the first note I had written all year to a girl; it would not be the last.) I wanted to go with her pretty badly by now, and I didn't want school to be have ended before she knew this fact. I felt that my chances were pretty good. I really wasn't worried about her saying "*No.*" And when she wrote me back the very next day, I felt even better. Then I read the note. Then I read it again. Technically, she didn't tell me, *No*, but what she told me introduced me to the true reality of future boy-girl relationships in high school (as well as in college).

I can't quote the note word-for-word, but what she basically wrote was this:

I was really touched by your note. You are a very sweet person and any girl would be lucky to have you as a boyfriend. I do like you and I wish we could go together, but right now, I am a couple of months pregnant, and my friend and I have to work this situation out. It would not have been fair to you if I hadn't been honest about this and not told you. I hope I didn't hurt your feelings and that we can remain friends.

After reading the note, I really didn't know how to react. I was surprised, yes, in more ways than one obviously. I was so naive that I didn't think girls who were around my age did *that* at that time. (Shows you how much I knew.) Of course, I was a little sad that we couldn't go together due to her condition and other circumstances beyond my control, but I also was happy because she did admit she liked me, enough to at least consider going with me. And that, friends, was one small step for relationships and one *giant* step for yours truly.

So after this enlightening experience, I was now ready to shed the "whatever-the-opposite-of-Casanova-is" label and become THE MAN (more or less). No more Mr. Shy-Guy. Now I was on a mission. When I became a junior, no one was safe. Even if I had to talk to every girl in the school (and believe me, I tried), I was going to have a girlfriend. For all the previous years where I didn't even attempt to talk to anyone, I more than made up for it my junior year. ("Hide the women! It's Don Juan!" – Devin) From September 1984 to January 1985, I was on a roll. I think the only girl I didn't try and talk to was Calacia, and only because she still intimidated me. Our lockers were right next to each other (go figure), and yet, I only said "hi" to her the entire year. But other than her, I was really out-of-control. I was talking to every girl I could (possibly) get my hands on. But in February, I finally slowed down after seeing for the first time this girl named Traci Richards. (I know whose name was in the chapter's title; be patient, we're getting to Kelly.)

Regression: Tuesday, April 2, 1985

It was in the main hallway in front of the library between 2nd and 3rd periods. I was headed towards class thinking about who to go after next when she walked right past me. I stopped dead in my tracks (almost causing other kids to crash into one another) and turned and watched her go by. Talk about (as Devin might say) a vision of loveliness! I was stunned. I mean, she looked _good_. She had long, black, curly hair, her skin color was a pretty dark-brown, her eyes were mesmerizing, her smile could melt steel, and her body was so fine, it was almost ridiculous. She had curves everywhere. I was thinking, *"What planet did she come from?"* Then I thought, *"Who cares!? She's next!"*

I wasn't thinking about whether or not she had a boyfriend or not; I was trying to figure out a way to meet her. I was thinking, *"Looks like it's time for another note."* But then suddenly, something happened.

Something not too good.

I turned back into Mr. Shy-Guy. (Oh no!)

Cold sanity had returned.

"There is no way a girl this beautiful and that fine is going to want to go with me, much less talk to me," I realized. It also occurred to me that she has to have a boyfriend; it would've been a crime if she didn't have one. No, I'd have to forget about Traci, and go on about my business. I had written her a note and had one of her friends give it to her, but now, I was thinking, *"Have I lost my mind trying to talk to this girl?"* I would have to be satisfied admiring her from afar like I did Calacia. I thought I would kind of have a hard time forgetting about her, and I did (Isn't it obvious?), but now someone else entered my sight.

Introducing Kelly Woodson: Monday, April 29, 1985

It all started this particular week. I was doing pretty well in my classes, I had went from being on the JV football team to the Varsity football team and spring practices were just beginning. Dave and I were still coming up with interesting ideas on how to make school better. Devin had broken his ankle during football practice and I was helping him get to some of his classes. And I was slowly getting over my discovery of Traci Richards.

I tried to concentrate on my studies as the end of school was nearing, but something kept nagging at me. I had reverted back to being a shy person, and I didn't like that. It just didn't feel natural.

Wednesday, May 1, 1985

School was turning boring and something was missing. (Guess what that was.) I discussed this with Dave over at his house this afternoon.

"Well, it's fixing to be the end of the year, and I still haven't accomplished everything I wanted to accomplish," I said.

"What do you mean?"

"Well, I wanted to make this year special--extra special. This was to be my "coming out" year. And I'm not saying it hasn't been. So far, anyway. But well..."

"You still haven't found that special person yet, right?" Dave knew what was on my mind.

"I haven't had a girlfriend the entire year! In fact, I've *never* had a girlfriend!" Incredible, but true. I'd come very close but little things such as shyness, jealous boyfriends, annoying little sisters and brothers, shocking pregnancies, and weird parents had always kept me from reaching my destiny.

I was reaching new and unheard of levels of frustration and I continued to vent: "And I tell you, it's disturbing when my little sister who hasn't even reached high school yet has had *two* boyfriends already before I've been able to even have one girlfriend. And yes, it's frustrating." Heck, it was super-frustrating because I was actually trying (kind of) to get a girlfriend, something I didn't do last year or the year before that, and even though I was shy, I hadn't been *that* shy. Not this year, anyway. And yet, my problem was...

"Your problem is you're trying to talk to girls who already have boyfriends." Dave said, "Think about it: LaShandra, Francine, Jocelyn, Messina, Valerie, Traci...we're talking "the cream of the crop" girls. It'd be a miracle if they *weren't* already taken. Why not try for someone you don't know? You know, someone you've never even heard of?"

Dave and I had been charter members of the "Lonely Hearts" club, but he finally was able to escape a few weeks earlier as he and Sue Lakely started dating then going together. This was *before* he and Carlina started talking. And Sue was a senior! So whatever ideas he had, I took to heart (my lonely one) and decided to at least try again.

So, I saw a girl in Dave's first period class that I was interested in getting to know. I didn't know her name, so the natural thing to do was to ask my buddy what her name was, right? Alas, Dave was absent for a few days at this time, so instead of waiting for him to come back, I decided to see if I could figure out who she was on my own. (This was Mistake #1.) Instead of being brave and using what little common sense I had left by just going up to her and asking her what her name was, I decided to look her up in some of my yearbooks. And based on sheer detective work and my above-average deductive skills, I decided that this girl had to be Kelly Woodson. (She looked like her picture.) So, when I wrote the note, I wrote it to "Kelly Woodson," meaning I put her name on the note. (This was Mistake #2.) I held onto the note until Dave came back to school, then when he did, I asked him did he know a Kelly Woodson. He did, since they had went to Forest Park Middle School together in the past. Then I asked him if he could give the note to her. Which, of course, he did. The irony of all this was (and this was the 3rd and final Mistake) that Kelly Woodson *was* in his first period class and he gave the note to *her*, but not to the _girl who I'd originally intended the note to be for_! Meaning that I'd guessed wrong the girl's name whom I wanted the note to go to. In one classical stroke, he gave the note to the "wrong" *and* "right" girl at the same time! In other words, wrong girl, right name. Or was it right girl, wrong name?

Anyway, it was also strange that during this time, I had no idea what had happened, and I kept hearing that Kelly wanted to meet me and that she was interested in me. But when I tried to approach "her," "she" acted as though I were invisible. Again, right girl, wrong name. Being that I was very confused, I was also confusing Dave, who probably thought I was trying to talk to two girls at one time. (Which probably wouldn't have been too surprising considering how desperate I was.) It would begin to clear up finally a couple of weeks before the end of school, when I heard that Kelly wanted me to meet her at her locker. During all this, Kelly knew what I looked like, but never came up to me because she was kind of shy herself. I still had no idea what she looked like for real as I was still thinking this other girl was Kelly. So I told Dave to ask her where her locker was (and I pointed to the wrong girl, of course) and Dave, though confused ("Are you sure?"), went and asked "Kelly" and she told him a locker# that was downstairs. *That's* when I first figured something was not right here. I was thinking, *"Only seniors have lockers downstairs; how did she get a locker downstairs?"* I went on anyway like a confused idiot to "her" locker, and when "she" again acted as if "she" didn't know me, I knew something was not right. Finally. (It didn't help either that "her" boyfriend was standing right there, also.)

After a long slumber, the light bulb finally clicked back on in my brain. I asked Dave just *who* did he give that note to in the first place. He told me Kelly Woodson.

Then I said, "Well then, who is that?" pointing towards the girl I thought was Kelly Woodson.

"I have absolutely no idea. Want me to go ask?" he replied.

"Yes! I mean...NO! I mean...that's the girl I wanted you to give the note to! That's Kelly Woodson, right?"

Then he corrected me and told me that I had asked him to give the note to Kelly Woodson, whom he knew, not the other girl, whom neither of us knew. (And to this day, I *still* never found out what that girl's name actually was. I thought she was Kelly Woodson, but she wasn't. It's a wonder I didn't completely make a fool out of myself.)

So in the final analysis, I had been after the wrong girl who already had a boyfriend for all this time while the girl who received the note was the right girl but the wrong girl to receive the note. She liked me, though, but I didn't know her. I thought I knew her, but it was the wrong girl whom I liked, who didn't know me. Confusing? Very much so.

So, back to the original question: <u>Who was Kelly Woodson</u>? I didn't have very much time to find out as the end of school was nearing. She had wanted me to meet her at her locker, but I still didn't know where her locker was. I wouldn't find out until the last day of school, which seemed to symbolize the saying, "To be so close and yet so far." A girl named Kayla Wiley told me she had seen Kelly reading a note I had written her and at the same time hugging a picture of myself I had sent with the note, so I asked Kayla to find out where her locker was. Kayla and Kelly were obviously friends, so Kelly gave her the locker number, and then Kayla passed it along to me. Dave had given Kelly my autograph book for her to sign, so I needed to get it when I met her at her locker. I still didn't know what she looked like; I had an idea but I really wasn't sure. But at least I had the *right* locker number this time, I think. (After all the mistakes I made, I wasn't sure about *anything*.) I was going to try to catch her at her locker after the final class and felt I finally was going to meet the "real" Kelly Woodson. But as usual, I screwed up. I got out of my final class late and had to hurry to the lockers. I made it to her locker thinking I was on time, but I wasn't. She had already left. And ironically once again, we *passed* each other right there in the locker area. (I wouldn't find all this out until later.) I was thinking, *"I've done it again."* But this time, I wasn't giving up...

The Chase Begins

Summer 1985

I'd known Ray Ross since our 6th grade days at Judson when we were both in Choir together. We talked so much that our teacher had to separate us. It didn't do much good; I then got placed next to Anthony Mack, who became one of my best friends while we were at Judson. Ray went to Forest Park after the 6th grade, so I did not see him again until we were in high school. Ray had always been a good guy, so I knew he would and could help me out as far as Kelly was concerned. He had mentioned to me before school ended that he knew where Kelly lived and it was kind of ironic (there's that word again) that they both lived on the same street, which turned out to be Younger Street, the street I had lived on back when

I was a child. It turned out she lived a couple of blocks down from Ray's house. It was sort of a dangerous neighborhood, but when it came to girls and meeting them (especially when I had never had a girlfriend), I didn't care if it was the worst neighborhood in the United States. I couldn't drive at the time (Well, I could, but why complicate things by having a wreck?), so I rode my bike over there, and on June 5th, 1985, I met Kelly Woodson for the first time.

She was cute, light-skin colored, had long hair and her face was serious, but friendly, with a nice smile. She was a little stocky but not fat, and very, very quiet. I liked her immediately, and her family was very friendly towards me. I thought I made a good impression on them, but I was wondering how Kelly felt about me. She was so quiet it was hard to tell. During the next few weeks, she encouraged me to call her, and in what may have been a mistake, I introduced her to my momma and sister. My sister thought she was nice, but my momma didn't like her. My momma really didn't like anybody as far as girls were concerned; she was being real protective, as usual. So it didn't really bother me to a certain extent. For a short while, it seemed Kelly and I was growing close, but then it all just faded away.

Part of the problem as I've mentioned before was my parents. My sister and I lived under very strict rules meaning we were basically under house arrest for almost the entire summer, with the exception being the trip to Port Arthur. I couldn't take the car anywhere on my own, and if I wanted to go somewhere, I had to ride my bike or sneak and go somewhere. And yep, when I did go to see Kelly, that's exactly what I was doing: sneaking over to see her. But it *was* fun.

However, my parents, namely my momma, started keeping a closer eye on me, and I couldn't get out too much. Therefore my visits to the Woodson residence were cut down drastically and I was limited to calling Kelly whenever I could find the time and opportunity. Needless to say, my parents kept me busy doing household chores, outside work, and making me prepare for my senior year *and* college by having me read and study *during* the summer. This was the one time where I completely lost interest in reading. Then I was also taking part in various church-related activities. I liked doing that; I just didn't like all the extra chores and work at home I had to do.

Then finally, in July, my sister and I went on our annual summer trip to Port Arthur to visit our auntie. As usual, we had a lot of fun without our parents, and as usual, we didn't want to come back home. We stayed for a couple of weeks, so that by the time we returned to Longview, I had forgotten all about Kelly. I didn't even try to call her. (I probably wasn't allowed to use the phone anyway.) It was back to the slave camp (not the ranch) and back to becoming a dull person again. As if I was going to let that happen. And I wasn't.

Even though I had not spoken to Kelly in a while, I had not totally forgotten about her. She was still on my mind as I entered my senior year. But then, of course, so were a few other girls. But Kelly was the one whom I could never seem to shake, the one I thought about constantly, and sometimes I didn't even know why. It would take me a whole year to figure that one out, and by that time, it would be too late.

CHAPTER 5

Kelly and Me, Part 2

Wednesday, October 9

So far, my week had consisted of trying to reacquaint myself with Kelly again by walking with her to her classes. She never complained or told me or asked me not to do so, so we were together almost every day. There usually wasn't very much said, and I imagine that some days, we really looked like an odd couple. We weren't going with each other (yet) though it wasn't because I wasn't trying; I just didn't know enough things to talk about to a girl who was way quieter than I was. Especially when I was trying to keep from sounding stupid. Usually I'd see her open up to her friends like Leslie, Randressa ("call me Randi"), Lorraine, or Theresa (they were all in the band together), but those times were not coming my way yet. Worse, Dave and Devin both felt like I was wasting my time trying to talk to her. I didn't feel that way. At least, not yet.

Thursday, October 10

I saw and spoke to Kelly again that Monday, but Tuesday and Wednesday, I didn't see her and I began to get the bad feeling she was trying to avoid me. I was about to give up when out of the blue, I heard someone say, "Hi Kelly." I looked around and saw Lorraine and Theresa, but I didn't see Kelly anywhere. *"I wonder who they're talking to,"* I was thinking, *"I don't see Kelly anywhere."* Then again, Lorraine spoke: "Kelly, what are you doing?" I looked around and she and Theresa started giggling. Then I realized that they were talking to _me_. "Why are you calling me 'Kelly'? We don't go together," I said, a little confused. "That's not what I heard," Lorraine said, "I heard you two were like two peas in a pod." Then Theresa added, "And we should know." With that statement, they walked away laughing.

As they walked off, I was trying to figure out what they meant by that. A couple of hours later, Dana Tolliver approached me and asked me did Kelly and I go together. Then Robrina Houston asked me the same thing. Then someone else. And someone after that. Finally, during my last period class, after Randi became the final person to ask the million-dollar question, I was almost convinced my own self that Kelly and I were going together, if not officially but willed by our classmates. I still hadn't seen her since Monday, but I felt like I had finally succeeded.

Friday, October 11

And guess what? I was very, very wrong.

I came to school, opened my locker, and found a note inside. It didn't have a name on it, only a message: *There's nothing much I can say except there could never be anything between us.* This was definitely not a hallmark moment, and I knew exactly who it was from. Or did I? The main question was: *Why? Did I make her angry in some way? Did I get on her nerves or did everyone else by trying to say we went together*?

Even though I shouldn't have been, I was down the rest of the day; I showed the note to Dave and he encouraged me by stating there were "plenty of other fish in the sea", so to speak, and Devin said basically it was her loss, not mine. As one could tell by reading this, my best friends weren't exactly too upset by what had happened and probably thought I was better off. As much as I wanted to feel this way, I couldn't. I felt as though I had failed in some way, and I didn't like that all-too-familiar feeling.

Tuesday, October 15

The rumors were swirling about Kelly and me. Such as, we had a fight and one of us was seeing someone else and so forth and so on. There still was a question of whether or not we were going together (which we weren't and never had), and if we were going to get back together or not. (Which wasn't possible since we never went together.) However, for once, I was able to smile about something for the first time since I received that hideous note from Kelly. The election for Homecoming Queen was going on at this time, and one of the nominees was Traci. Another nominee for the title was Calacia. They were two of the toughest girls around, if not *the* two toughest. Traci wanted to know if I was going to vote for her or not. Between her and Calacia, that was going to be a hard decision, and I guess in order to sway my vote, she gave me a very nice and long (and very needed, also) hug. It was the kind of hug which made me wonder why I was so upset with Kelly's note in the first place. Like Dave said, there were plenty of other fish in the sea. I told Traci I'd definitely vote for her.

Friday, October 25

It was a strange week. I felt like I was popular with just about everyone except the person I wanted to be popular with. For some strange reason last Friday, I had asked Kelly (who, remember, didn't want to have anything to do with me) if I could call and talk to her over the weekend.

Yes, I obviously had taken my stupid pills that week, but I didn't give up. Surprisingly, she said yes. Then not so surprisingly, when I did call, she wouldn't or couldn't come to the phone. Not knowing the meaning of the word "surrender" (or the meaning of the words "stupid fool"), I kept trying to talk to her. It just wasn't registering with me that she just didn't like me. Strangely, every other girl in the school was speaking to me, getting me to do different things. Nothing bad, mind you. Traci had spoken to me three or four times that week. That in itself was cause for a small celebration. Wendy wrote me a short note. Michelle Brownlow asked me to keep her books for her. Randi had been trying to get my attention all week during Spanish class. Weirder than weird: Tina Robbins, one of the Viewette leaders and someone who did not have any trouble getting guys' attention, wanted me to get her a corsage for Homecoming and she gave me a tin of do-nuts and a hug that Friday before the game. I told Devin, "I must be in the Twilight Zone." And still, for some stupid reason, I still wanted to go with Kelly. Go figure.

Homecoming Week October 28: November 1

Monday, I walked with Kelly to her classes and we seemed to be trying to patch things up and get along. Maybe she saw all the attention I was getting from the other various females and got jealous. Yeah, right. The next day, I went on ahead and ordered a corsage for her to wear on Homecoming. Obviously, I felt that no sacrifice (goodbye comic books) was too great in order to please the girl I loved(?) and cared about, so despite some lingering doubts, I continued on. Of course, Dave thought I was crazy, Devin said I was a fool, and my sister, Flower-child, put a sign on my bedroom door which stated '*There's a sucker born every minute – W.C. Fields.*'

There was going to be a Homecoming dance after the game, so I asked Kelly if she wanted to go to the dance, but she never really gave me an answer. By that Thursday, I had changed my mind about going to the dance anyway. My parents were probably going to have something to say about that, so I forgot about it.

Friday arrived, the day of Homecoming, the day of the BIG game with John Tyler for the district championship, and the day of reckoning for Kelly and me. I hadn't been this excited since Christmas. I waited until 4th period to give her the corsage, and when I arrived to her class, someone spoke to me as I entered the classroom. This person spoke in a very sweet, sexy, and familiar voice (and it definitely was NOT Kelly): "Hi, Cedric."

I looked around and saw who it was. And I thought, "*Oh my God, Traci is in Kelly's class this period! Dang, she looks good!*" I quickly cleared (and cleaned) my thoughts and I mumbled hello. As if I wasn't already nervous enough, Traci's presence and speaking to me did not help me at all. I had imagined myself presenting Kelly with her corsage with the grace and the presence of a true gentleman, but instead, thanks to Traci, I felt like Humpty Dumpty. As usual, Traci was looking very fine, but I had to focus, focus, <u>FOCUS</u>! Forcing thoughts of Traci away from my head, I saw Kelly and feeling kind of awkward, I presented the corsage to her with Traci watching the whole time. Kelly accepted it with somewhat of a smile (she was surprised), and as I got ready to leave, Traci again spoke in a sing-song sexy voice: "Bye, Cedric." I glared at her, this time with a small amount of irritation. Any other day I'd be on cloud nine, but not today. Why Traci was being so friendly now I'd never know and it was making me sick. I looked at Kelly, who also kind of glared at Traci, then we said bye and I quickly left the room.

Later, I walked with Kelly to her fifth period class, and she was a lot friendlier and happier than she had been the preceding weeks (and preceding hour). She really did like the corsage and was very surprised I bought and gave her one. We talked as if things were going to be a whole lot better in the future, as if we were really going with each other for real, and as if those good feelings were going to last forever. I actually believed this. Again, I was wrong...

Monday, November 4

The note read, *Again there's nothing I can say except there can NEVER be anything between us!* Again, it was stuck in my locker sometime that morning, and even worse, I shared my locker with my sister, and she had seen the note before I did. And she wasn't too happy about the note. (She loved her big brother-how sweet.) But once again, Kelly broke my heart. This time, it was more shocking than the last note because I kind of didn't see this one coming considering how well we were getting along the Friday before. In fact, I wasn't quite sure if Kelly wrote the note or not because at first it didn't look like her handwriting. (It was scribbled in meanness.) She didn't sign her name on the note, either. I asked her the next day did she write the note and she admitted to doing it, but somehow I still couldn't believe it. Maybe I was in denial; I don't know. It took a while (about a week or two), but I accepted it and I figured I had spoken to her for the last time. But time has a way of healing old wounds, and the year wasn't quite over yet.

CHAPTER 6

Devin's Song

Wednesday, November 6

One thing I could say about myself: I might be down but I ain't never out. Not totally anyway. But I was in somewhat of a morose state at the beginning of November after receiving the note from Kelly. Micheal had shown me a picture of his new girlfriend from Dallas, and though I was happy for him, I was down for myself. One thing about having good friends, though: They notice when you're not exactly feeling great and they try to pick your spirits back up in some form or fashion. Sometimes they meant well; other times you wished they'd leave you the heck alone. Micheal gave me a pep talk about not giving up, of course; Dave encouraged me to try and try again. ("For someone else." He added.) He hadn't totally abandoned his "machine-gun theory", and he didn't want me to give up either. And then I had another one of my teammates try to solve the problem directly by trying to set me up with someone he knew. Harold Loyd and I were pretty good friends from the Judson days, and him being the friend he was, he decided to take matters into his own hands. He told me he knew this ninth-grader (??) who liked me a lot (from a distance, of course) and wanted to get to know me better. Even to the point of us going together, like, right now. He didn't have a picture of her or anything like that, but he said she was real fine and kind of cute. I told him I'd think about it (Yes, I'd heard beggars can't afford to be choosy, but I wasn't a beggar.) and I went home and asked my sister did she know the girl Harold was talking about. I kind of figured she would since they both were in the same grade. She did, and so I asked her how did she look? "She looks alright, I guess," Flower said without much enthusiasm. *"Oh Oh,"* I thought, *"ugly girl alert."* Buzzers and alarms went off in my brain. "You could probably do better, or even worse. Really, it's your choice whether or not you want to talk to her. She's kind of strange but not as strange as Kelly." My sister sounded as if she didn't care what I did, as long as it wasn't stupid and embarrassing to her. She had been sharing my locker here lately and had seen the note in my locker and wasn't any more happy about it than I was. But she really didn't tell me what I should or shouldn't do, so I was on my own.

I really had to concentrate here. On one hand, I wanted a girlfriend. On the other hand, I didn't want just anyone. I had my "picks" just like everybody else. And though Harold probably meant well, you don't never set anyone up with someone who looks better than your own girlfriend, if you know what I mean. And Harold had a very nice-looking girlfriend. Also, as I've stated before, I preferred older girls to younger girls, as it was hard for me to be interested in someone younger than me. Every girl I had talked to in the past had been older than me, with the exception of just one, Vanessa Henderson, who also happened to be in the same grade as my sister, and who was someone very, very special obviously. But that just wasn't meant to be, just like this one. (More on Vanessa later.)

So, for the next few days, I kind of tried to avoid Harold. I didn't want to look like I didn't want or appreciate his help, but for a while, it was futile. I saw him just about every day, and each time he would ask me if I had talked to his friend yet. I'd make some lame excuse to keep myself from doing so. You know, like 'Well, not yet. I'm still waiting for so-and-so to get in touch with me,' or 'I've had too much homework and blah, blah, blah...' And so forth and so on. Finally he figured out I wasn't really interested in the girl and went on his way trying to find someone else to go with her. He had a hard time doing that I'm sorry to say, so I guess I made the right decision for once.

Friday, November 8

As usual, Devin had me laughing about other things that didn't have to do with girls, and as fate would have it, he would have the whole school in an uproar this day with the exception of yours truly, who happened to be throwing up that morning at home. Devin figured the pep rallies needed a bit more spicing up and he decided to do something about it. It had been a tradition for a member of the football team to get up and say a few words about the upcoming game, something along the lines of, *Tonight we play the Mavericks. Please come out and support us and we'll bring home a victory.* Or something similarly dull and uninspiring. (Believe it or not, and I have to mention this because it was a classic, when we was at Judson, we had to do the same thing. One particularly interesting Thursday (Middle school football games were on Thursdays), the cheerleaders called up Willard Thomason to say a few words about the upcoming game. And when I say he said a FEW words, then that's exactly what he did. Willard was usually a quiet person and basically said sentences which contained four or fewer words. Like "Hello", and "Where are you?" or "My toes hurt." You get the picture. Well, Willard got up and this is exactly what he said: *"Tonight we play Marshall White. They might want to fight."* Then he sat down. The entire student body of Judson

Middle School as well as the entire Blue Devil football team went <u>wild</u>. (And yes, we went out and beat the daylights out of Marshall White, who *did* want to fight, but not play football.)

This time it was Devin's name the cheerleaders called out to speak to the student body. Devin got up and went to the microphone and at first, nobody noticed anything unusual.

But I guess the twigs sticking out of his pockets were normal.

I suppose him holding a couple of pine combs didn't mean much either.

Then he spoke and normalcy officially and quickly ended.

"Tonight we play the Pine Tree Pirates. I got a song I want to sing about that and here it goes:" And with that, Morris Day's *"Oak Tree"* started playing, but with different words and a different singer. (Again, I missed all this; Devin gave me the whole story afterwards.) Believe it or not (and I still don't), Devin sang and rapped a song called "Pine Tree" in front of the whole school! And it went like this:

> *Pine Tree, we'll put you to the test*
> *Pine Tree, when it comes to football, we're the best*
> *Pine Tree, we're shutting all the doors*
> *Pine Tree, when it comes to winning this is how it goes*

Oh. My.God. An old tradition perished (somewhat) that morning and a new tradition was born: *We're not only going to talk about what we're going to do to these teams; we're going to sing and rap about it too, and then go out and kick their butts.* In later years, Lobo players would do that more and more, and we can thank (or kill, depending on one's perspective)

Devin for that. I thought it was great because it livened up the pep rallies (which, ever since they started taking place mornings instead of afternoons, they were sort of dying out) and fired up not just the team but the whole school. Still, it was strange for Devin, of all people, to get up and do that since at this time he was still as quiet as the proverbial mouse, at times. It was strange, period, for him to even be selected to give the "we're gonna take names" speech because he might would've probably given one of those quick, boring, coach-like speeches just to get it over with instead. And even stranger was that I somehow, incredibly, sadly, and any other negative adverb you can think of, missed it. (Yes, that really *killed* me.) I must have been really, really been sick that day, on a game-day at that, to keep me from going to school.

Devin told me that the whole entire gym went crazy. And of course, we shut out Pine Tree that night, 16-0.

Monday, November 11

When I came back to school Monday morning, I had no idea what Devin had done. My mind and body was still trying to heal itself of the virus *and* Kelly, and I was in Neverland. Micheal brought me out of it, though, as we sat at the table during first period.

"Boy, you missed one helluva pep rally. That had to have been the best one this year."

"Yeah, right," I mumbled, still under the influence of medication.

"Can you believe what Devin did?" asked Ronnie.

"Man, was he hyped up!"

I looked at them and asked, "What did he do?"

"What? You weren't there?" said Ronnie.

"Where?" I said, totally lost.

"He wasn't there, man. He was sick," said Micheal.

"Oh, that's right. You were absent Friday. Your boy showed out at the pep rally."

I was starting to get the sinking and sickening feeling that I had missed out on something special. "What do you mean?"

Micheal said, "He did a song and dance to *Oak Tree* except he called it *Pine Tree*. You know, I didn't know he had it in him, but it was LIVE!"

"You know it," said Ronnie.

"He did WHAT??" I could feel the meds wearing off and the nausea returning.

They all told me the same thing second period. Devin rapped. And *danced*. "I don't believe it," I said, "he doesn't even know how to dance!" (Actually, Devin *did* know how to dance; he just never did it in front of anybody.)

I still didn't believe it until I finally got to talk to "James Brown" himself during third period. "Yeah, I did it," Devin bragged, "I was scared at first, but once I got into it, it was all over with."

I kicked myself. "How in the world did I miss that?" Now I couldn't believe I missed seeing him do that, and it seemed I was the only one in the whole school who didn't see it. Then Devin added, "Don't you remember last week I asked you to write a song for me to use at the pep rally? They told me they were going to call me up to speak during that pep rally so I'd have time to prepare. Remember?"

At that very moment, I vaguely remembered him saying something about that the week before, but I hadn't done what he asked because I had been so caught up in Kelly and plain forgot about it. A brief flash of anger went through me as I thought about the time and money wasted trying to impress Kelly.

"Yeah, yeah, now I remember."

"And you didn't get to see me perform?"

"No, I missed it. I was probably the only dummy that did." I could just hear my sister's voice about learning from a dummy.

Devin smiled. "Good," he said, "at least one person didn't get to see me make a fool out of myself. That's all I've been hearing, *"Boy, we didn't know you had it in you,* and *Devin: Live from the Pep Rally."* People have been coming up to me, people I don't even know, and they've either been congratulating me or mocking me. "I guess I'm not ever going live this down. But at least I won't have to hear anything from you."

I said to Devin, "You didn't make a fool out of yourself, brother. I'm the one who's the fool, and in more ways than one." Then as I walked back to my desk, I said to myself, *"I just can't believe I missed that."* And I probably was never going to live <u>that</u> down.

CHAPTER 7

Changes in November

My journal entries during the month of November were very brief- with the exception of one entry about a Jodie McClure memory. I also left out some of the entries about our varsity football team as those entries have a chapter all to themselves. These were what my entries looked like, with the addition of personal thoughts in parenthesis:

Friday, November 1

Today I gave Kelly the corsage and it really surprised her. I think that she really likes me now. (Boy, was I wrong.) She told me we'll be seeing more of one another. And the best news of all, we beat John Tyler 7-3 to become the District Champions!

Sunday, November 3

I went to Sunday school, church service, and B.T.U. (Something I normally did back then was go to church all day; I liked it.) I really didn't want to go to B.T.U. though, because I wasn't feeling too good. (I thought I was coming down with a cold. Actually I was coming down with a virus from Friday night. More on this later.)

Monday, November 4

Yes, I got a note from Kelly, and no, it wasn't a good note. She hated me for some reason and now it was over. Micheal showed me a picture of his new girlfriend he met from Dallas, and she really looked nice. I was happy for him but sad for myself. I'd been encouraging Micheal to get to know his new friend better and it paid off for him very handsomely. Too bad I couldn't say the same for myself.

Tuesday, November 5

I thought that Kelly had lied to me about writing the note, but she actually wrote it. Also, some girl's paper was stuck in my locker. It was some sort of worksheet she had been working on, and why it was in my locker, I don't know. I asked Flower about it, but she didn't know anything either. (This would happen three more times during the year from the same girl, but I never tried to find out who she was.) My cold was getting worse.

Thursday, November 7

Today I literally and figuratively blew up (and threw up). I came to school looking worse than ever (according to my buddies, who should know), I forgot some of my books and left them at home, I had a terrible football practice during fourth period (I actually got into it with some of my teammates over something inane), and I basically got sent home. I went straight to bed.

Friday, November 8

Even at home, absent from school, things went wrong. Not only did I miss the football game against Pine Tree, but I missed Devin's coming-out performance at the pep-rally. I couldn't seem to find anything at home and couldn't seem to stop throwing up. And no, I didn't get much sympathy from my parents, either. The only thing I did noteworthy was watch my favorite show at the time (and one I hadn't seen in a while because of Friday-night football games), *The Dukes of Hazzard*. And speaking of *The Dukes of Hazzard* and football:

The Dukes of Hazzard, Football, and Dana Tollive: January, 1979

In January, 1979, a new show debuted on CBS called *The Dukes of Hazzard*. With its car chases, country atmosphere, and pretty women, it became the most popular show to watch among us kids back then. We thought Bo and Luke were cool, we loved us some Daisy Duke, and we all wanted to own the General Lee someday. Never mind about the Confederate flag on top of the car or the horn which played "Dixie," we would want to drive the orange car anyway and we were *black* kids. All the stereotypes, the racial implications, and the history surrounding the Civil War didn't register with us back then. We just loved the show. I made sure I watched it every Friday night. It was my favorite show at the time. (When Bo and Luke left the show one year, I nearly died.) Life back then was watching Dukes of Hazzard, playing football in the front yard, and being chased by Dana Tolliver. Two were cool, one was not-so-cool.

I was a football-junkie by the spring of '79. I lived and died watching the Dallas Cowboys on TV. When they won, everything was good. When they lost, it was painful. I hated when they played on Monday Night Football because for one thing, it seemed they usually played terrible on Monday nights. Second, I could never stay up to watch a Monday Night game, I always had to go to bed at 9 p.m. The next day, when I would wake up and find out they lost the game, then that pretty much ruined my day right there. I had gone from having magazines and posters to having a Cowboys jacket, stocking cap, and bag. But probably my most prized possession was a Nerf football I had gotten for my birthday. Our front yard was never the same after that.

Everybody came over and we would have some hellacious tackle football games. There was Joe Sealy and Dennis Todd, who were a couple of Flower's classmates, the Hensley twins, the Simms twins and their brother Will, who was my classmate, Ron, Marvin, Charles, George Tracy, and of course, Thomas and Charlotte. (Tackling Charlotte was fun.) It was great. The yard didn't look like it could hold a bunch of kids, but back then, it looked like a giant field. We didn't hold back from each other either. We tried to knock one another out. And we did have our fights. Joe and I fought a lot, because he tackled too aggressively. He really had fights with just about everybody because of his tackling, but we always got along even though we would fight each other. One time he tackled Flower-child in a really rough way and I didn't like or appreciate it and let him know it. Next thing you know, we're rolling down the hill fighting. Joe, Dennis, and Thomas had a small brawl at one time while I stood there laughing at them, and once Ron and I had a small skirmish. I only recall getting hurt a couple of times, once by Joe and another time by my cousin Vern. Joe, even though he was 2 years younger than me, was big for his age, and one time he really drilled me to the ground on my left shoulder. I swear my shoulder was actually separated. I had to go in the house and try to pop it back in place on my own without Momma knowing. When I did pop it back in place, I nearly fainted from the pain, but then it didn't hurt no more and I went back outside and kept playing. Like I said, I _loved_ football. The other time I got hurt somewhat seriously was when my sister and I were playing our cousins, Vern and Christopher. Christopher was younger than Flower, and Vern was older and bigger than everybody, so they were on a team. Christopher threw Vern a pass which he caught, and he took off running upfield. I was running to meet him and we collided…BOOM!! Vern went flying one direction, the ball went flying another direction, and I went flying in all directions. I felt like I lost body parts all over the yard. I picked up my head and carried it into the house, done for the day. Vern later told me that was the hardest he'd ever been hit and that it was a good tackle. To me, it felt like I had tried to cover a live grenade. I was hurting for days after that collision.

The 5th grade girls at Jodie McClure could've been a football team all to themselves. These girls were not your dainty, girlie, sugar-coated type females; these girls were big, tough, and taller than most of us boys. They would fight you and make you think twice about trying to pick on them. Being the boys we were, we would of course throw caution to the wind and agitate some of the girls on purpose, because we actually liked them. (We couldn't tell them or anyone that, however.) We were still considered little kids, but we still had our moments. One day, we had a major boy-girl fight outside on the hill on the side of the school. It was boys versus girls, and though it wasn't serious and mostly for fun, things were getting kind of hectic out there for a while. In other words, we boys were on the verge of losing the brawl. The toughest girls out there were Tangie, Rena, LaSandra, Kim, and Dana from my class, and Shelia Mars, Brittany Walls, Cheryl Pearson, Estella Jones, and Zelma Jones from the other 5th grade class. Though we were mostly paired up with girls we (didn't) liked, I was going after three or four girls at different times because I guess I couldn't make up my mind which one I (didn't) liked. Then, it just so happened that it looked like Dana was getting the best of my buddy, Marvin, so I quickly ran and jumped on her back and took her down. She was mad (happy?) about that and tried to get me, but by then, it was too late and time to go back into the building. I guess she took me jumping on her like that as akin to me marking my...uh...space, and though I forgot about it, she never did. A few weeks later, it was time for PE, and since it was raining outside, we had PE in the cafeteria. I was the first person coming in the cafeteria, as I had gotten a headstart from everybody else...but one person. The next thing I knew, someone had jumped me from behind, turned me over, and had me pinned to the ground. Guess who? The worst part was that she wouldn't let me up until the whole class had come into the cafeteria and seen me in this predicament and let their minds go crashing into the gutter. I guess she had "marked" her territory by tackling me. From then on (at least, until the beginning of the 6th grade), it was "Dana likes Cedric" or "Cedric likes Dana." On her end, that might have been true. On my end, I did like her, but as a friend, not a boyfriend. But that didn't stop her-she sat by me in class, sat by me in the cafeteria, talked to me all the time, came by my house (she stayed right down the street from me), and really put more fear in me than she would ever know. I thought I was ready for girls, but Dana showed me I wasn't.

Saturday and Sunday, November 9-10

I stayed home the entire weekend. The rest of the family went to Shreveport Saturday and everyone went to church Sunday. I stayed home and watched a football game (Dallas beat Washington, 13-7, the only good thing that happened over the weekend), and I pondered the events of the past week. No Kelly, and worse, no comic books. (Thought I was kidding about the comic books, huh?)

Monday, November 11

Today I felt miserable. Miserable from the virus and miserable from missing out on seeing Devin rap at the pep rally last Friday.

Wednesday, November 13

Harold told me he's trying to set me up with this girl. I didn't know anything about her except that her name is Sharon. Devin mentioned to me that he thinks Annette likes me. I didn't think so. (This was the first time Devin mentioned this; it would not be the last.)

Friday, November 15

Today we left for Dallas for our playoff game Saturday against Killeen Ellison.

Sunday, November 17

Today, after getting home at 4 a.m., Momma made get up at 8 a.m. and get ready to go to Sunday school. I was not happy about that, but on I went. Then during church service, I fell asleep on the back pew at the back of the church, and got in trouble when our pastor informed Momma what I had done. I only got to see probably about five minutes of Dallas' game with Chicago; it was just as well: they lost 44-0. I went to sleep.

Tuesday, November 19

Another "great" day: First, Momma is still fussing at me about Sunday; Second, the English test was hard; Third, I got caught copying in Calculus; I didn't get into any major trouble; Mr. Double C could see that my notes weren't going to do me much good anyhow and I probably got the grade I deserved. Fourth, I missed the bus. No biggie. To me, anyway. To my parents however, it was like I had committed a murder. Fifth, my parents (who were on a roll here) were still fussing about "college night" and my seeming disinterest in it many moons ago. (I really should have been interested in that-since I did want to go to college after I finished high school, but what can I say? My teenage mind was on other things.) And sixth and last, my grades were trying to drop. Again, what could I say? It was all Kelly's fault!

Wednesday, November 20

Devin told me again today that he thinks Annette likes me. I was still not all that certain. We had been talking to each other a lot lately, though.

Thursday, November 21

Another boring day. The only highlight (if you can call it that) was we got to see Flower perform on "Honor America Night" with the freshman band. Flower-child had been kind of quiet during this time. She was using my locker at school and not really being any kind of a pest. I guess she felt I was going through enough as it was.

Friday, November 22

I was really falling for Annette Ray. She was a very nice girl, and her looks weren't bad, either. She had nice medium-length hair, chocolate brown skin, dark brown eyes, and a smile that could melt glaciers. She was very petite, fine, and ultra-friendly. And I loved her southern voice. She asked me to keep her book for her before the team left for Waco today and she gave me a hug. Of course, that felt good and made me feel good. I needed that.

Sunday, November 24

Of course I went to Sunday school and church service. This time I was prepared despite returning from the game around midnight. And I watched Dallas beat Philadelphia, 34-17. They always seem to play pretty good around Thanksgiving. Too bad we (as in the Longview Lobos football team) didn't.

Friday, November 29

Annette and I wrote each other today and I asked her if she wanted to go with me and she told me yes. We called each other every day and once (Wednesday) we talked on the phone for two hours straight. Thursday, of course, was Thanksgiving, and my family and I had turkey, dressing, potatoes, green beans, rolls, cake, and sweet potato pie. (I hate sweet potato pie.) I watched Dallas beat up on the St. Louis Cardinals, and I talked to Annette on the phone again. This time, my parents got on to me about being on the phone too much. No surprise there. The next day, we travelled to Fort Worth to visit some relatives. I didn't really enjoy the trip as I missed Annette the entire time. I couldn't wait to go back home.

Flower said she hadn't see me dislike a trip so much since the last time we went to Ft. Worth back in 1984. I probably set the record back then for the most Kleenex used in one day I was so congested. We didn't do *anything* close to fun.

Sunday, December 1

We went back home today (Finally!) and guess who called me as soon as we got home? Annette, of course. She was so much different from Kelly, she was like a breath of fresh air. It's GREAT to be home!

CHAPTER 8

Annette and Me

Friday, November 22, 1985

I didn't see it coming. I really did not see it. Devin said he saw it coming maybe a month ago. He said he could see that there was an attraction between me and someone whose name wasn't Kelly. Or Traci. Or Rena.

"Brother," he said, "I think Annette really likes you."

"No way," I thought to myself, *"Annette does not like me, and besides, I like Kelly."*

Then Kelly put that note in my locker, and I was in her life no longer. I began to converse more with other girls in my classes and obviously I had been conversing a lot with Annette during our third period Economics class. Even more interesting was the fact she had been talking to me a lot more here lately also, not just in class but in between classes also. *"Could it be? Nah!"* I quickly shoved the thought aside and figured Annette was just being friendly, that's all. I didn't want to overreact, so I continued playing the "lonely man."

Then Devin noticed that Annette and I had been not only talking more during class, but looking at each other a lot during class also. I would say that was his imagination, but the fact was I had been watching Annette a lot here lately, and I liked what I was seeing. She started getting me to come over to her desk and help her with some of her work, and as I'd mentioned before, Mr. Polawski had to get on me for hanging around her desk too much.

("Stop being a Don Juan or something and sit down at your own desk!")

Now, after Devin had said what he'd said, I did find myself being attracted to her, but I didn't think she actually felt the same way. And at this time, I really wasn't trying to go with anyone or chase after anyone or anything like that. I still was trying to get over Kelly and that stupid note.

It didn't take long.

One day, Annette got a hold of my Economics book and wrote me a note on the front of my book cover. She basically said she wanted us to talk more and get together more often. And she wanted my phone number.

Ding! I saw the light: We had been talking a lot and she did seem to like me a lot. And I obviously liked her a lot, because all I could think about was her. How quickly we get over people like what's-her-name?

On Friday, November 22nd, our football team got ready to leave for Waco for the playoff game. Before we left, Annette asked me to keep a book for her, wished me luck, and gave me a very nice hug. I was surprised, to say the least. We looked at each other, and I admit I probably turned red, but the thought hit me like a brick: I was in love.

Tuesday, November 26

The following Tuesday, after talking, calling, and writing to each other, we made it official: We (drum-roll please) decided to start going together.

Annette Ray was my new girlfriend. (Yes!)

Kelly who?

It was kind of hard to believe that when I first met Annette, we were in the ninth grade and she was in my Homemaking class. I figured she was one of those loud, fast girls from Foster Middle School (not that there was anything wrong with that, mind you) who would highside you in a second and laugh about it for an hour. And I figured there was no way she would ever be interested in someone like me because I was too quiet back then. Well, she might have been a little loud (at times) and a little fast (just kidding, she wasn't), but she was one of the nicest and sweetest people you'd ever meet. Not to mention she was very cute and nice-looking. She had long black hair, had a nice dark complexion, a pretty smile, and a nice petite figure. It was hard not to fall for her. But what really was shocking to me was that she seemed to like me just as much as I liked her. We wanted to be around each other, not just one person wanting to be around the other, if you know what I mean. And after dealing with the unemotional, ultra-quiet Kelly Woodson for the past few months or so, this was like a breath of fresh air. It felt good to talk to someone who actually cared about what you were saying instead of either ignoring you or looking at you like you were crazy, and that is what really made our relationship.

To me, she was the perfect girlfriend. We were like two good friends; we talked to each other about anything. And we called each other a lot. When my family and I went out of town for Thanksgiving, she called me before I left and called me as soon as we got back. I had never had any girl do that before, and it made me feel pretty good.

During Christmas, she became the first girl I had ever bought something and given to for Christmas. I think it was a nice purse and pocketbook set and she really appreciated the thought. The thought would get me in trouble later with my momma, unfortunately.

One day, Devin and Annette decided to play a little joke on me during our lunch period. They played like Devin was me, and I was supposed to be Devin. Annette was the first to call Devin and me "the twins" because she said we acted like we were brothers since we were alike in so many ways. OK, whatever. As I sat there and they kept acting like I was Devin, Devin was pretending to be me and Annette also was pretending Devin was me by really playing the girlfriend part. She was sitting very close to me, er...I mean Devin, almost hugging him and calling him Cedric and acting like she was whispering something in his ear. I was like, *Whoa, wait a second here. What's really going on?* Then they laughed and everything went back to normal. She asked, "Were you jealous?" I laughed, "Who, me? Of course not. I knew y'all were playing. That was a good one. Ha Ha." Actually I didn't know whether to be happy, mad, sad, or what, so I just laughed it off and convinced myself it was a joke. Which it was. Devin, even though he went along with the joke, had started looking uncomfortable and hadn't really wanted it to go too far. Annette and I continued to get along great and we stayed friends for a long time even after we finally broke up.

Question: Why did we break up?

Answer: Nothing lasts forever.

Seriously, all I can say is, it simply wasn't meant to be. (Now where have I heard that one before?) I liked Annette a lot, and I'm pretty sure she liked me a lot at the time also. But we really could go no further than being just real good friends. I think that sometimes, deep down, it could have been something more, but it just wasn't meant to be. And to be fair, she really liked someone else even more so than me, and they wound up going together for a long time, even after we had graduated. But we continued to talk to and call each other afterward every now and then, and sometimes I thought we might would go together again someday.

But it would never happen.

She was never mean to me unlike someone else I knew, and I appreciated her for that. At the end of December, we weren't going together, but we were still friends.

Meanwhile…Back at the Ranch: Wednesday, December 4

Momma had been leaning on Flower and me pretty hard here lately about our grades, our study habits, being on the phone, and almost everything else. And it was starting to reach a boiling point.

Saturday, December 7

The parents went to Shreveport to shop and left Flower and me at home. They came back fussing at us about the house looking bad. It didn't look that bad, but with them, everything wrong we did was tripled in their eyesight.

Sunday, December 8

I noticed that I wrote down we went to church as usual, then after church, we went to Marshall to visit our pastor and his wife, which was unusual. I didn't care too much for our pastor at this time, and his wife was obviously very, very weird. Her bathroom was all mirrors--on the floor, ceiling, walls, everywhere, and to say she liked looking at herself would be a total understatement. We had a real good pastor before this one showed up, and I don't know how or why he became our pastor. Our former pastor and the one who baptized me, Rev. J.H. Hillsdale, was one of the nicest and kindest men one would ever meet, and he was a GREAT pastor. (And of course, he was Vanessa's daddy.) It was a SAD day when he left. But this pastor we had now, well, he just wasn't a real good pastor. A lot of times he didn't feel like preaching a sermon, at one point getting up and saying his wife and he were not getting along and that he just wasn't up to preaching the word that day. I wanted to walk out. And his wife, she looked like she fell off the turnip green truck a few too many times. And we went to go see these people. Another miserable day.

Monday, December 9

Today I had a dumb spell; I made a 58 on one test (probably Calculus) and a 47 on another test. That was probably Spanish, which was no big deal anyway since she usually dropped the lowest two grades every six weeks. I could afford to have a lapse in that class. But not in Calculus.

Tuesday, December 10

During fourth period and lunch, Tony Mack and I talked about the "good 'ol days" back when we were at Judson Middle School. Anthony definitely was my best friend back then, and even though I hadn't seen him too much since we entered high school, we still were good friends. We talked about the races we used to have (back when I was fast), the "toss-up" football games, the electronic football games we used to sneak to school, and all the times we used to make fun of and talk about girls. (We couldn't talk too much, however.) Anthony was one of the fastest guys in school (probably in the top three) and I always used to give him a run for his money. I probably beat him once or twice, but that's about it. He had speed on top of speed. He would've been a great running back or a superstar in track, but he went a different direction. Still, it was good to reminisce about those days and as he got up to leave, he said, "Later, *'Fleetwood Mac'*." That's what he used to call me at Judson.

Thursday, December 12

Dave told me he was going to stop by my house and visit afterschool, but unfortunately, I had to stay afterschool and help clean the Homemaking rooms. Obviously, my mom was probably subbing that day for that class and Flower and I probably had to stay and help her straighten the room out.

(Yes, we had janitors back then but I don't know what happened there. We might have been being punished for something.)

Monday, December 16

Today I got my schedule changed for the second semester, due to start in January. Good news: Instead of varsity football, I was going to be in Radio-TV. This was historically a very fun class and an easy "A" if one was creative. Bad news: I got two progress reports. Parents predictably hit the ceiling.

Tuesday, December 17

Annette wrote me a note on my book wanting me to talk to her more, which was something I hadn't been doing here lately because I felt like I had got on her nerves last Thursday. And I had really needed to concentrate on my school-work more, anyway. But she didn't have to tell me twice. We sat together during lunch.

Wednesday, December 18

We (mi familia) went Christmas shopping today, and I had no trouble getting something for Daddy, Flower, and Annette, but Momma was altogether a different story. She was in one of those moods again; she didn't like anything we (my sister and I) picked out, so we wound up getting her nothing, which really made her angry. I don't know why we all went together. Like most things back then, we probably had no choice. But the whole evening was stupid, and Momma was especially mad at me because I got Annette something and not her. I couldn't win for losing.

Christmas, 1985

I gave Annette her gift the Friday before Christmas and she liked it. She gave me a card which I thought was nice and I appreciated it. However, the days leading up to Christmas were marred by Momma who had turned into a total Scrooge for the season. Momma decided to punish me one day by making me rake all the leaves outside front and back plus do all of the chores around the house, which Flower had to do the one thing she hated doing: dusting all the furniture. I had bought Momma a Christmas present earlier but she said she didn't want it.

Sunday came, and church was terrible, as usual. Momma's attitude had grown worse (if that's possible), and my attitude was starting to worsen. Flower and I asked Momma for a soda, she said Flower could have one but I couldn't, as if I had not been punished enough. I was a very unhappy camper.

Then on Christmas Eve, Momma, Flower, and I rode to Tatum and went out to eat. The day was only notable (and memorable) in that Momma and I didn't say more than five words to each other the whole day (it been that way the last few days) and Flower got real sick after eating and Momma either didn't care or seem to even notice. I thought for sure Flower was going to lose her lunch right there in the backseat, and then we didn't even go straight home! We went to go visit the Queen's, and from there, Flower took off running home. I followed, but only to go get my bike and go see Annette, who wasn't home.

Finally, mercifully, Christmas came. This would be the first Christmas of many where I wouldn't care what I received; it was the giving that mattered. I got clothes, shoes, and a jam-box, but I was happy to be able to give a present to Daddy and Flour (and Momma, even though she said she didn't want it). What I really wanted to do was go see Annette, so I left the house to go visit her. But once again, she wasn't there. I left her a note letting her know I came by and rode back home.

Sunday, December 29

Today was my parents' anniversary but the day was anything but celebratory. By this time Annette and I were just very good friends. I wished we were more but I was happy with that. However things at home were anything but jovial. Momma's month-long "Midol moment" continued, as she and Daddy got into an argument about church and the anniversary itself. Then again Momma fussed at me about the Christmas present I gave Annette. I got frustrated and angry and stayed that way for the next couple of weeks.

Fast Forward To: Wednesday, January 8

My feelings finally boiled over. Momma, who at the time, would have probably enjoyed beating a dead horse into the ground, *once again* brought up Christmas and accused me of spending too much time with my friends, calling them and so forth, and spending too much time on my computer. (Which, incidentally, I was using to help me with my schoolwork.) Then Daddy accused me of something I didn't do. Flower may have tried to say something, but either they wouldn't let her or they just weren't going to listen. I finally just got tired of everything. They grounded me, but I didn't care. I had had enough. I was ready to leave home and never come back.

This story continues in Chapter 10. The next chapter is my favorite chapter because it's about…

(Turn the page)

CHAPTER 9

The District Champions

Note: This chapter is dedicated to one of the greatest teams in our high school's history, if not the GREATEST. (OK, so what if I'm biased?)

The Year Before: Friday night, November 16, 1984

The final score was Bryan 24, Longview 14.

What's that old saying: The game wasn't as close as the score indicated. In my four years at LHS, that was the longest (in more ways than one) and coldest game I've ever experienced. It wasn't supposed to end this way. A first-round playoff game (at home, no less) against a team we were supposed to beat real easily, the first in our quest to become state champions. We were considered the NO. 1 team in the state at the beginning of the year and were favored throughout the year to win our district. We had the best running back in the district (if not the state), the best defense, a very good quarterback and receiving corps, and a solid kicking game. There was no way we weren't going to win state, much less district, bi-district, area, and so forth. Devin and I and the rest of the juniors on the team felt fortunate and real good about our chances of being State Champions before we became seniors. We could almost smell it.

Obviously, our noses were out of order.

That game was the only one ever I did not want to participate in, and I wasn't the only one. I stood by Devin most of the time on the sideline, watching the seniors and a few of the juniors who played take a beating. Bryan had come to play and they came to take names while doing so. I thought Texarkana and John Tyler hit hard, but they didn't come close to how Bryan was handling us. What made it worse, besides the fact that we were getting beat in front of our own fans at home, was that it was a very cold night. And with each touchdown (or field goal) scored by Bryan, the night grew colder and colder. By the 4th quarter, it felt like the Ice Bowl or something. The stadium and our sideline were ominously quiet. We were beaten, and we and everybody else knew it. The quarter seemed to take an eternity. We were frozen (mentally and physically), and we were very, very flat. I hate to admit it, but I was glad when the game ended. The final was 24-14, but it felt more like 74-14.

We went into the locker room, which in some ways was as bad (or worse, if that's possible) as the game itself. It was so quiet in there that it was frightening. The seniors on the team were very upset and angry about that game since it was their last game, and they were basically ready to fight anyone who said anything about the game and about how we played. The coaches understandably were angry about the lack of fire and intensity on our team for this game, but with the season being over, there wasn't much they could do about it at that particular time. The rest of us were upset also, but for us, our feelings were tempered by the thought and relief of knowing there was always next year.

Friday, September 6, 1985

Longview 17, Eastern Hills 0

After all the practices, predictions, and preparations, we finally played our first game. This time, there was no doubt we were ready to play. Nothing was going stop us, not even a driving and steady rainstorm, which we got during the game. But the bad weather didn't matter; we won easily, 17-0. Our quarterback, Corey Carter, played real well, throwing a touchdown pass to our top receiver, "Fast" Freddy Woods. The running game was stout, led by Cleve Loyd and Terrell Scott, who got over a hundred yards between them. But the main story was our defense. Led by seniors Tank Thomas, Jonathan Cobb, Don Champion, Joseph Johnson, Gary Morris, and Marlon Ames, the defense totally shut down Eastern Hills, thus establishing their season-long trend of dominance from the get-go. If it hadn't rained so hard, I was pretty sure we'd have scored more points. But all-in-all, it was a great way to start off the season.

Friday, September 13

Trimble Tech 21, Longview 17

Friday the 13th.

What more needs to be said?

Except, so much for our goal of winning all of our games.

The day itself had not been a good one for me personally, then it kind of carried on to the game. As far as the game went, we started off great and finished poorly. Trimble Tech had never beaten us before (I don't think), and at first, it looked as if that streak was going to continue another year. We were running and throwing the ball with ease, our defense was shutting down Trimble Tech as if they were babies, and there didn't seem to be any way we were going to lose. We were up 17-0, and Devin, Daryl Jackson, a junior guard, Rollo Raines, a junior wingback, and myself were prematurely talking as if this game was already over. Rollo was very exuberant, to say the least. "Party at my house tonight!" he yelled.

It was still 17-0 in the 3rd quarter, and we were threatening to put up more points on the scoreboard. But then, weird things (this being Friday the 13th remember) started happening. Devin gave me his goggles while we had been on the sidelines after complaining about them half the night, and he went back in without them. His prescription goggles, which he needed them to see with. Devin played wingback and a play-action pass was called where he was to take off deep down the right sideline. Needless to say, the play nearly was executed perfectly. Devin was wide open with no one around for yards, and Corey threw a perfect pass which hit Devin squarely...on top of his helmet. The crowd groaned as the ball hit the ground. Devin claimed later that he couldn't see the ball due to the lights. Actually, without his prescription goggles, he might as well been blind. Then, after he dropped yet another pass, we just about had to force him to put the goggles back on.

Suddenly, we all started playing terrible. Trimble Tech rallied to score three touchdowns, two of them in the fourth quarter on the same play; a slant pass thrown to a receiver who broke our cornerback's tackle both times and ran it in for scores. The last score came with little over a minute left to play, and after we couldn't move the ball for what felt like the 20th time that half, the clock ran out, and we, incredibly, had lost to Trimble Tech. This meant there would be practice the next morning, a long-running tradition we did not want any part of.

Friday, September 20

Abilene 3, Longview 0

Talk about a surreal game. For some reason, during the entire game, I felt like we just were not meant to win this game. We had the ball constantly in Abilene territory, only to kill ourselves with penalties, sacks, dropped passes, and fumbles. It also didn't help that we missed three field goals during the game which could've made a difference. Abilene missed two field goals also, but made the important one with 1:30 left to go in the game. We drove back into field-goal range, but with 10 seconds left, we missed our final field-goal and again ended up losers. Like the Trimble Tech game, this game was at home, and again, we lost at home.

The defense deserved better.

Especially Tank, who played like a man possessed, and Gary, who made another interception and ran it back all the way to the 1-yard line. Then we promptly blew it by committing another penalty, giving up a sack, and missing the field-goal. As great as the defense played, the offense didn't really match the defense' play. We couldn't do anything right. And as far as the missed field-goals went, the normal holder had quit during the past week, so me and this other guy had practiced alternating holding for kicks. I didn't do too bad during practice, but during the game, it probably made a difference. Our coach, Coach Douglas, was not very happy, of course, and the week ahead figured to be one of...well...hell.

Friday, September 27

Longview 14, Tyler Lee 3

We had heard it all week:

"What's wrong with Longview?"

"Longview is doomed!"

"The worst team in Lobo history!"

"It's time to get a new coach!"

We were going to be playing at home again, and the fans as well as the students did not think we were going to do too much. I was thinking differently, however.

It was what it was-a butt kicking. Despite the seemingly deceiving close-looking score, Tyler Lee was never really in the game. Again, the game wasn't nearly as close as the score indicated. Major stat: Longview had 225 rushing yards, Lee had 149 *total* yards. Our junior tailback, Terrell Scott ran for over a hundred yards and scored a touchdown, and our senior fullback, Cleve Loyd ran for 70 yards and scored the other touchdown. Our kicking game was still a bit shaky as we missed an extra-point and a field-goal, but the defense, which had been in an ugly and surly mood since the latter stages of the Trimble Tech game, continued to make opponents pay for even thinking of advancing the ball on them. Tyler Lee had been 2-1 in non-district action (this was the first district game) and supposedly had a very good defense (nicknamed the "Rambo Defense" after the Stallone character; yeah, right), but compared to our own "Mean Green Defense," it was strictly no contest. We were establishing more trends, such as stopping teams on fourth down, which we seemed to do two or three times a game; blocking field-goals (the third straight game we had done so); and holding teams to under 200 yards total offense.

It was also the first time I didn't worry about Tyler Lee being any kind of a threat during the game (even when it was just 6-3 in the third quarter), and I think we all felt that way. Especially after being criticized by just about everyone, put down, and downright laid to rest the entire previous week. We could now spread the news: The Lobos are alive and well and we're 1-0 in district!

Friday, October 4

Longview 20, Texarkana 0

As our busses rolled into an obviously older section of Texarkana and into Grimm Stadium (aptly named) and its parking lot (if one could call it that; I swear we had to drive through someone's yard to get to the gravel-covered parking lot), Devin tapped me on the shoulder and declared, "The butt-kicking tour continues!"

Last week, we had wanted to set things straight. This week we felt we owed Texarkana something for last year's game (which they had won, 6-0, on a cheap, undeserved touchdown), and by the end of the night, the debt had been paid in full.

By the time we had gotten finished defeating the Tigers, showered and gotten dressed, and went out to eat at a place called Doc Alexander's (which had excellent hamburgers, by the way), we had:

1. Rolled for 249 total yards on offense, 181 rushing, 68 passing.
2. Raised our record to 3-2 for the year, 2-0 in district.
3. Held the preseason favorites and reigning district champions to 185 total yards.
4. Collected 3 fumble recoveries and an interception.
5. (Another trend) Held an opponent without a touchdown for the third straight game.

6. Scored on a pass and a run and two field-goals.

Cleve scored yet another rushing touchdown, and (hurray) Devin got one on a pass. He was finally forgiven for dropping those passes in the Trimble Tech game. We went home feeling great about ourselves, but also realizing the best was yet to come.

Friday, October 11

Longview 10, Nacogdoches 0

Actually, the best wouldn't come in this game, but at least, we won.

That was almost all that could be said. This game was at home and it should've been a total blowout.

It wasn't.

This was an ugly, putrid game. Really, it was beyond ugly. Nacogdoches (a town I'd really become familiar with in the future) had not won not a single game up to this point and could almost be excused for its paltry showing (only 94 total yards for the entire game). But we nearly put the entire stadium to sleep, gaining only 108 total yards ourselves. In the first half alone, we only had 10(!) total yards of offense. Not good. Like in the Abilene game, we kept killing ourselves with stupid penalties and ill-timed sacks and turnovers. Unlike the Abilene game, however, we had almost no offense. Nacogdoches' defense was very, very stout and they totally shut down our running game, not an easy thing to do.

Fortunately, we still had our kicking game, which had gotten better and better, and of course the No. 1 defense in the district. Our kicker-punter, Jake Barlow, had his best game, making a field-goal, keeping the Dragons at bay with great punting, and making a touchdown-saving tackle on a kick return. We also blocked another punt, which set up the game-clinching touchdown. Then there was the defense. I knew if I had to face Tank, Jonathan, Joseph, and company, I'd take off in another direction. I thought Will Stanton, our starting linebacker last year, was crazy, but Tank was beginning to make Will look sane by comparison. The Dragons tried to go for it on a 4th and 1 early in the third quarter, but didn't make it because Tank nearly took the runner's head off his shoulders with a vicious hit in the backfield, and he screamed a scream that was spine-tingling, like the hit itself. (What is with these teams trying to go for it on 4th down so much? They must have thought they had Earl Campbell Jr. in the backfield or something.)

One last thought: Four straight games, no touchdowns allowed. Enough said.

Friday, October 18

Longview 24, Lufkin 10

Out of all the teams we had played up to this point, the Lufkin Panthers and their fans were definitely more fired up about this game than anybody else we had played. We could feel the electricity in the air before the game started. I could say that Abe Martin Stadium (the home of the Panthers) was rocking, and I'd be telling the truth. They were doing something, and they actually felt their team was going to win this game. But of course, we knew and felt differently. Despite our having lost our starting quarterback to an injury, we still won the game by a couple of touchdowns. The juniors on the team played particularly well, thus giving our district something to look forward to next year. Lufkin did score the first touchdown on our defense in 17 quarters, but other than that, they were pretty much shut down like everyone else we had played. We scored three touchdowns in all, one on a run, two on passes, and on one of the passes, our speedy receiver, Freddie, made a spectacular diving catch in the left corner of the endzone which had to be seen to be believed. It occurred right before halftime, and interestingly, it had occurred a play after Devin should've scored on a trap play we ran only to be shoestring-tackled by the only Lufkin defender who saw the play coming. (Yeah, Devin was very upset about that. It would've been about a thirty-yard touchdown run.) But Freddie's play just about took all the air out of Lufkin, and they were no longer a threat the rest of the game.

We were now 4-0 in our district with three games remaining. We were obviously headed towards a showdown with the only other undefeated team in our district, the John Tyler Lions, for the district championship. But first, we had to get past the Marshall Mavericks, our next opponent. We had defeated them 17 straight years dating back to 1968, so it was almost hard not to look past them to John Tyler.

Almost.

Friday, October 25

Longview 42, Marshall 12

And it wasn't even that close.

Marshall didn't put up much resistance as we ran over them (and "ran over" was exactly what we did, having rushed for a total of 305 yards for the game). It definitely was our best game of the year. For once, we played a total game in front of our home crowd. We scored six touchdowns, four on runs, one on a pass, and one on an interception return. Again, the juniors on the team played great. Carl Grimes had taken over for Corey at quarterback in the Lufkin game, and he had continued to play well. The two Terrells, Terrell Scott and Terrell Stone, ran with authority, scoring four touchdowns between them. And our junior cornerback, Darrell Richards, ran the interception he made back 80 yards for a score.

Of course, we seniors on the team did pretty good also, and Coach Douglas was more than satisfied with the results. Now as Devin and I walked off the field, we knew it was time for the big one. John Tyler was running roughshod over everyone in the district and out of the district. They had not lost a game to anyone period (they were 8-0, 5-0 in district) and were giving the Pine Tree Pirates, the other Longview school, a beating the same night we were demolishing the Mavericks. They were scoring over 30 points a game and seemed to be unstoppable. Our next game was going to be for the district title. Now the pressure was on.

Friday, November 1: Homecoming Game

Longview 7, John Tyler 3

As we stood in the tunnel waiting, I felt something I had not felt all year: total and absolute fear. Fear of losing the biggest game of our young lives. Devin and most of the others felt it, too. There wasn't any talk of "butt-kicking tours" or anything like that before the game; we just wanted to survive and win the game. This was going to be pressure to the fifth power. This was our Homecoming game, so the stadium was packed to overflow. Not only were we playing in front of the entire school, our parents, our sisters and brothers, our grandparents, our girlfriends, our friends, and other various relatives and fans associated with the Lobos and its history, but also the game was to be televised live on channel 7 throughout the East Texas region (a rarity in those days). So just about everybody was going to be watching this game one way or another, watching to see if you were going to be a hero, or if you were going to totally screw everything up. Speaking for myself, I was as nervous as a long-tailed cat in a room full of rocking chairs. I think we all felt like we needed a lot of coffee. But what we really needed, and wanted, was a win.

At 10:40 p.m., it was over.

The winner and new 1985 District 13-5A Champions: The Longview Lobos!

What a game.

It was one of those games where there shouldn't have been a loser. It was a hard-fought, emotional, clean game for both teams, who each gave it their best shot. The defenses of both teams dominated the game, but in my opinion, there were only two things that made the difference in a victory for us and a defeat for them: 1. Our defense was a shade better than their defense. And 2. Our offense scored the only touchdown of the night on a trick play which hadn't worked in practice at all.

John Tyler did move the ball some in the second and third quarters, but our defense consistently came up with big plays to stop their drives. We made a couple of interceptions, forced them to kick a field goal after they had a first-and-goal at our eight-yard line, and stopped them on a fourth-down and three (there these teams go again thinking they're going to make that) from our 10-yard line.

After the Lions had kicked their field-goal, which occurred in the second quarter only seconds before halftime, we faced a second-down and 10 from our 38-yard line. There was around 20 seconds left before half-time, and the coaches decided it was time to spring the trick play we called the "Texarkana Special." It was named so because we had planned to use it against Texas High earlier, but didn't because it had never worked in practice. So we saved it for this particular moment when the pressure was definitely on. (Kind of ironic in a way.)

We hadn't done much if anything up to this point on offense, so we needed to do something. We needed a spark. What we got was the biggest play of the season. (And maybe of the decade…ok, maybe not, but it felt like it.) Our quarterback, Carl, took the snap and fired a backward pass to the wide receiver/split-end which bounced once off the turf before he caught it. This was to make it seem it had been a bad pass and a dead play when actually it was a backwards lateral. Gary Morris, our starting safety but playing split-end on this play, then took the ball and lofted a perfect spiral to Freddie, who was all alone about forty yards downfield. Freddie caught the pass at about the 25-yard line and outran the Lion secondary all the way to the endzone with just seconds to spare. The crowd went crazy. Our football team went crazy. It was a great play with great execution by everyone involved. We went into the locker-room at half-time feeling good, but still nervous. In fact, speaking for myself, I wish I could say I knew we were going to win the game from that moment on, but I'd be lying. In a sign of things to come for me personally, I had an attack of diarrhea during half-time, which kept me in the locker-room a few minutes after the third quarter started. (My stomach never got back right the rest of the game; I'd make a return trip after the game ended.) We had to protect a

7-3 lead, and our defense was up to the challenge, no doubt about that. Time and time again, we snuffed out John Tyler's chances of scoring and possibly winning the game with big hits and timely sacks. The defensive front line of Jonathan Cobb, Joseph Johnson, Don Champion, and Johnny Bails (all seniors, of course) played probably its best game. They dominated JT's offensive line to the max. On John Tyler's last drive of the game, they got three sacks, all in a row. Game over.

When the clock ran out, the entire stadium (with the exception of a few unhappy John Tyler fans) stormed the field. Everybody was celebrating, screaming, dancing, hollering, the works. Because believe it or not (and not many people did or thought we were capable at first) the 1985 Longview Lobos were District Champions! We still had one more game left to play against our cross-town rivals, the Pine Tree Pirates, before going on to the playoffs, but we were going to savor and enjoy this victory as long as we could. Myself, I was going to start by enjoying it in the bathroom.

Friday, November 8

Longview 16, Pine Tree 0

Remember the diarrhea attack from last week? Well, that turned out for me to be the beginning of the flu virus, which in turn caused me to be absent from school Thursday and Friday, and caused me to miss the game against Pine Tree, which we won rather easily. We scored two touchdowns and a field goal, all in the second half, and held Pine Tree and their dangerous running game to 200 yards total offense. Terrell Scott had a big game, breaking for several big gains and scoring on a long touchdown run thanks to a great block by my buddy Devin (that's what he told me), and the game was merely a formality afterwards.

Now we were headed for the playoffs as the district champions, with our new goal being becoming the State Champions. We felt we had the team to do it, and our first-round opponent was going to be Killeen Ellison. In a dream come true, we were going to be playing at the home of America's Team, the Dallas Cowboys, meaning we were going to be playing at Texas Stadium next Saturday. There wasn't going to be any first-round early exit like last year; this time, we were going to be ready for the challenge.

Saturday, November 16

Longview 17, Killeen Ellison 0

Yes, of course we won the game (Was there any doubt?) Fast Freddie scored on two touchdown passes including one thrown off a double-reverse pass. (We loved our trick plays, especially when they worked.) Jake kicked a long field-goal, and the defense was just totally awesome. Wicked would be more like it. Donnie Champion, Jonathan Cobb, and Tank Thomas practically lived in Ellison's backfield all game long. And on the special teams, Gary Morris and Marlon Ames were spectacular, blocking two field goals and setting up the offense with a long kickoff return at the beginning of the third quarter. However, the day and evening was made memorable by what happened not only during the game, but before and after the game as well.

Though our game was to be on a Saturday night, we departed LHS the day before via two charter buses. We left around noon, so we got to miss a couple of classes, which was nice in itself. One of the classes I got to miss was Calculus, so I was doubly blessed. As we made the trek westward to Dallas, one of my favorite cities, I had brought with me a small portable TV (as well as a miniature camera, which would prove to be very useful later), so Devin, Kevin Johnston, Daryl, and I watched television as we traveled. (Of course, we watched cartoons.) We made into Dallas just as everyone was getting off from work, so we were caught in a traffic jam for maybe an hour or so. (Yep, the TV came in handy.) By the time we got to the hotel and got unpacked and settled in somewhat, it was time for us to go again. We were going out to eat and also out to Texas Stadium and watch some of the other playoff games which had been scheduled that evening. We really had a good time; it was almost like being on a trip or a vacation or something. We tripped out at the restaurant we ate at, making fun of some of the customers and how they were eating and looking, and of each other, as we tried to see who could out-eat whom. (I ate just enough to keep me satisfied.) Then we went out to Texas Stadium. For some of us like myself who had never been to Texas Stadium before (despite being a hardcore Dallas Cowboys fan at the time), it was a great experience. We got to walk around the entire stadium, take in the sights (girls, of course), eat some more food, and watch part of a playoff game. I was going to take some pictures, but something inside of me told me to wait until the next day. (Good thing I did.) We weren't paying too much attention to who was playing (the coaches were doing a little scouting), and I couldn't tell you who was playing that evening. We were only concerned about our own game and having as much fun as we could. Which we did, in spades, when we got back to the hotel and started clowning around, wrestling one another, throwing things, etc., until we all finally went to sleep.

The next morning, after we had all woke up, cleaned ourselves, and gotten dressed, we all met in a giant dining room. Predictably, we were all expecting a giant breakfast with all the fixins'. What we got was, well, the opposite. All we got (on a paper plate, no less) was some grits (I hate grits), one sausage apiece, a hard biscuit, and some runny eggs. We couldn't believe it. It kind of reminded some of us something that happened the year before. We were getting ready to play Eastern Hills or Trimble Tech or some team like that, and we were having our traditional pre-game meal after school. Usually the coaches would take us to the Butcher Shop or someplace like that, but for this game, we were going to be eating at the school, and we heard and were told we were going to be having steak and potatoes and all the trimmings. Many of us including myself upon hearing that bit of news decided to skip our lunches in order to save more room for the steaks. (Yeah, not very smart.) We almost couldn't wait for the pep rally to end (for once I wanted the pep rally to last about two minutes), and when it did, we practically ran to the cafeteria and sat down. We waited for about 10-15 minutes, then after a while, they started rolling the food in on carts in covered dishes. We all started drooling like animals until they lifted the lids off the dishes. Then we started reacting like animals that had been shocked by cattle prods when we saw what were in those dishes. All we got for our pre-game meal that infamous day was what boiled down to being nothing more than hamburger meat smothered in gravy and some mashed potatoes. That's it. To add insult to injury, the potatoes and gravy were cold, and it was that fake hamburger meat they put on the school hamburgers. Needless to say, we didn't eat that crap, and we took it out on whomever we played that night, winning by thirty points.

Anyhow, back to the present. We were all unhappy about the crappy breakfast, and we stayed unhappy until we went out to the stadium for practice. It was my first time standing on the artificial turf of Texas Stadium and I was totally in awe. Before we started practice, we all walked around a bit to get a feel of the turf. I took the small camera I had with me out of my warm-ups and started taking pictures. Then, something incredible happened: The Dallas Cowboys themselves came out of one of the tunnels and began to go through a walk-through practice right in front of us! We all just stood there in shock as they did a few laps around the field, and then ran a few plays. Some of them even spoke to us. There was Tony Dorsett, Danny White, Bill Bates, Dennis Thurman, Randy White, Everson Walls, Mike Renfro, Tony Hill, and even their legendary coach, Tom Landry, came out there for a little while. All we could do was stare and look mesmerized. Myself, I reacted at first by standing there with my mouth wide open until Devin whispered, "For crying out loud, Ced! Take some pictures!" After looking at him like he was crazy or something and going, "Huh?" I finally remembered what the small object in my hand was for and I started taking pictures. Of course, nobody minded (some of my teammates were already offering me money for the pictures), and Everson Walls himself spoke to me and wished us luck in our game. (Ironically, the Cowboys were getting ready to play the Chicago Bears, soon to be the 1985 Super Bowl champion Chicago Bears. The game did not turn out too well for Dallas--they lost to the Bears the next day, 44-0.)

From that moment on, practice, our pre-game rituals, and the game itself went swimmingly well. The game had started slowly, but by the middle of the third quarter, we had taken the game over. We were not going to lose our first playoff game like last year's team had done, and I think we proved we were not flukes, either. We won the game convincingly. After the game, we had a huge celebration. We all went back to the hotel, and along with the band, cheerleaders, Viewettes, and other various family members and friends, we had a feast fit for a king. (Or fit for a winning football team. I guess they were making up for that pitiful breakfast.) We had everything imaginable known to man for consumption by mouth...chicken, chicken-fried steak, spaghetti, baked ham, potatoes, green beans, peas, lasagna (Which, before now, I had never tried before. And it sure was good, let me tell you!), bar-b-q, corn, hot rolls, cakes, pies, and the works. I had never eaten so much at one time before in my life. And I thought I probably never would again, either. That thought lasted a week. It truly was a GREAT night to be a Lobo.

Saturday, November 23

Cy-Fair 14, Longview 7

All good things must come to an end.

I kinda had a feeling it wasn't going to be a good week right at the beginning of the week. We had left Dallas around 1am and came back to Longview at 4 o'clock Sunday morning. I went to bed at 5 o'clock that morning, and three very short hours later, my mom woke me up and told me to get ready to go to Sunday school. Needless to say, that was one of the last things I wanted to do at that particular moment, but Momma being

Momma would not hear of me staying home, so I had to get up and go on, unhappily and very, very tired. To add to my chagrin, Flower didn't even have to go to Sunday school or church because she was sick. Was I missing something here? That kicked off the week right there. Our game was going to be in Waco this week, at Baylor Stadium, and for some reason, we just could not get excited about the upcoming game with Houston's Cypress Fairbanks. The whole week during practice, we were flat as I don't know what. The coaches were somewhat concerned, but they felt we would snap out of it.

Unfortunately, they were wrong.

We left again on a dreary Friday afternoon and made the even-longer trip to Waco. I think I slept half of the trip. We sort of got lost in Athens (the highway signs were confusing), but finally found our way and made it to Waco that evening. We didn't go anywhere that night; the hotel we stayed in had a small, nice comfortable restaurant, so we ate there. Then we went back to our rooms and had a quiet night. (Some of us that is. A few of the guys had some interesting visitors. But that's another story in itself and probably best not told.)

The high point of the entire trip occurred Saturday morning. We all had congregated to the giant dining room the hotel provided us expecting a meager breakfast like the one we had last week, but instead we got the direct opposite. We thought we had ate a lot last week, but I think some (if not all) of us broke the record this time. This time, we had a breakfast fit for a king. And for his queen, his subjects, the serfs, and the royal jester. We had an unlimited supply of bacon, sausage (all kinds), eggs (scrambled, sunny-side up, and boiled), hashbrowns, grits, rice, pancakes, waffles, toast, French toast, ham, pork chops, and anything else one could think of having for breakfast. The whole football team ate and ate and then ate some more. If it hadn't been so good, it would've been ridiculous. Some of us had between seven and ten helpings. As incredible as it sounds, we just could NOT stop eating. I stopped counting after my fourth plate. I was sitting with Devin, and if I was looking half as miserable as he was looking after we had definitely over-done it, I didn't know how we were going to make it through a football game, much less be able to push ourselves from the table. The coaches were probably going to have to roll us onto the football field. The game had been scheduled for 2 p.m. that day. I looked at my watch, and it read 11:30 a.m. At that moment, Devin, myself, and possibly two-thirds of the team could not get up from the table. We were so full that if we had tried to move an inch we would have probably exploded. I told Devin, "I, uh, think we're in trouble." Devin, looking and feeling like he weighed 1000 pounds, replied, "I think you're right. Oh well, pass me some more bacon and sausage, please."

By game time, the pigs and chickens had been fattened and were ready for slaughtering. (Yeah, I'm talking about us.) Somehow, we made it to the game, and from the start, we looked terrible. We scored on a long touchdown run by our quarterback, but that was it. Cy-Fair wasn't really a good team, and they were just begging for us to beat them, but we wouldn't oblige. We kept them in the game by playing extremely uninspired football. Actually, the defense played great, as usual, but on offense, we were lethargic. It was tied 7-7 in the third quarter when we tried the double-reverse pass which had worked in last week's game. When it works, it's great, but when it doesn't, it looks like hell. This time, it backfired miserably as Cy-Fair intercepted the pass (which resembled a thrown bean bag), and scored shortly thereafter. We spent the rest of the game looking totally inept, and though we had a couple of chances to at least tie the game, we just could not make any plays. When the final gun sounded and we had lost, a wave of depression swept the team. Then, on a smaller scale, there was relief. Last year, there had been mostly anger. This year, there was mostly sadness. We had lost to arguably an inferior team by a 14-7 score which could've gone our way easily if we had been a lot more fired up. Or if we hadn't ate so much before the game. I think we all kind of regretted that. I know I did. But too, there was relief and pride in a job well done because a lot of people didn't expect us to be that good, or to even be district and bi-district champions, which we were. I think we did a very good job of upholding the Lobo tradition of champions, and I was proud to be a member of that '85 team. We all were.

CHAPTER 10

When I Was Young

Wednesday Night: January 8, 1986

I was trying to go to sleep, but I couldn't sleep. I was really frustrated with a lot of things, and having a hard time trying to sort everything out. I was tired of living at home in that atmosphere, but I had no idea what to do about it. Correction: I had some ideas but they weren't good ideas. How did all of this come to this at this particular moment? I laid there and started thinking about the past, when I was just beginning to see things differently from the way I did when I was a little boy…

My Name is Joseph: December, 1978

Back when I was attending Jodie McClure Elementary, we had a music period which was usually around 10:00am. We would usually sing different songs, or we learn about different musical instruments and how to play them. Came December, our music teacher got the class in order and told us we would be doing a Christmas program complete with a Christmas play. The play would be about the birth of Jesus. She started handing out parts, and when she gave me my part, she said that I would be playing Joseph. The rest of the boys nearly fell out from laughing and started picking on me instantly. At the time, I didn't get it. *"What was so bad about playing Joseph? And worse, who was Joseph?"* Not trying to be funny, I only vaguely knew the story of Jesus' birth at the time; the church we had attended previously when we lived in Longview before had been a Methodist church, and they preached mainly from the Old Testament back then. We hadn't really attended any churches in Abilene, and we were only a year away from attending and joining St. John Baptist Church. I had it explained to me by Marvin what was Joseph's contribution to the story of the birth of Jesus Christ, and I, still not totally getting it, began to wonder was I going to have to hug and kiss my wife, or carry her across the stage? Slowly but surely, I started to get stressed out. Then I came to find out that this play was going to have a Black Joseph and a White Mary, since Dela Barnes, who was really a nice and sweet girl, was playing Mary. There was a little trepidation about that as we practiced, but it quickly passed as I worried about just playing the part period. Another minor issue was that me and the guys playing the three shepherds would all have to carry big sticks as staffs, and we would all race to grab sticks because one of the sticks was way taller and heavier than the other three. One would have to be Superman, or Moses himself, to be able to hold that big gigantic stick up. I was actually supposed to have the larger stick, but I had to push a large wooden donkey and try to hold that stick up at the same time, and it was not the easiest thing in the world to do. A bunch of times during practice, I'd grab one of the smaller sticks and leave one of the shepherds to suffer holding the leftover log from Abe Lincoln's cabin.

Finally, on the day of the actual program, my momma decided it would be best for me to wear my 3-piece suit to the program. (Shaking my head.) I had to put on my robe costume over the suit, and when I say I was hot, I was roasting in all of those clothes. Then I forgot to grab one of the smaller sticks, and the shepherds left me Moses' staff for me to fight with during the program. When the curtain opened, I was struggling carrying the large stick and pushing the wooden donkey which was as tall as I was, and on top of everything, I'm burning up with four sets of clothes on. Then I looked at the audience, and saw Momma and Daddy-I was shocked to see Daddy there, because he didn't usually miss work, and I was really happy to see him. After that, the only thing which bothered me was that I was sweating like a hog, but other than that, I felt great! I made it through the program, learned more about the birth of Jesus and the true meaning of Christmas than ever before, and got to run home before school was out and change clothes, then come back to school. That was a first. So, it ended up being a good day.

Toss-Up, Blue Devil Style

September, 1979

In September, 1979, I became a Blue Devil. I started attending Judson Middle School, which was about 5 miles north of Longview, and felt more like 100. I would spend the next three years making more new friends (and enemies), going through my first official crush on a girl, struggling with certain classes for the first time in my life, going to school without Flower-child for the first time, and discovering what true hell is all about: riding the big, yellow bus. Riding the bus was an adventure in itself. Either you rode it standing up the entire trip, or you rode it fighting somebody all the way home. I did my share of both during my first two years at Judson. So did a lot of my classmates.

There was the time when Tank Thomas and Tony Mack almost got into a fight during a game of toss-up. Toss-up was a game similar to touch football except there were no teams; it was every boy (and sometimes girl) for himself. You played by throwing a tennis ball or football up in the air, grabbing it or catching it, and running in the direction of the endzone before you got touched (or tackled, if we were playing tackle). If you didn't get touched, then it was a touchdown. Basically, it was makeshift football to keep us kids from getting too bored. We usually played out on the concrete in the center of Judson Middle School. We played touch most of the time, but sometimes we would (very stupidly) play tackle. (Just imagine getting tackled on concrete.) Sometimes we had a ball, such as a tennis ball, a plain rubber ball, or a small football, or sometimes we had paper rolled up into a ball, or sometimes aluminum foil paper rolled up in the same way. All the boys who wanted to play would play, and one also saw some tough tomboyish girls such as Rosetta Johnson, Tina Robbins, and the afore-mentioned Dana Tolliver and Rena Mack, who would play. There could be as many 30 or 40 kids playing at one time. And it was fun.

At times emotions would get the best of us, especially that year when it seemed there was an average of three fights a day. I remember Tank pushed Tony out of bounds rather forcefully to say the least, and Tony slid and fell to the concrete ground. Instantly he was ready to fight, and Tank, who could be somewhat of a bully back then when he wanted to be, was not backing down. Fortunately, they were separated before things got totally out-of-hand. It would not be the last time Tank would push somebody down like that. He got into three or four fights that year, mostly on the bus. Back then, there was a fight everyday on the bus. There were 80+ kids who rode the bus, and it was crowded, hot, and uncomfortable. There were bullies who rode the bus, and probably the worse were a couple of *girls*, the Darnell sisters. They terrorized boys and girls alike and would fight anyone. Many a day went by where they got thrown off the bus for fighting. One of them really seemed to make it a point to pick on Charlotte every single day, and they had a fight just about every day. My momma, of all people but not really surprisingly, was the one who put a stop to that when the girl bully was about to fight Charlotte in our front yard. Momma was basically saying, "Not today", and that ended that because Momma didn't play.

Another interesting sixth-grade memory was the time I met Velecia Stanton. Why was this interesting? When I was in the sixth grade, I had first period Advanced Math, second period Advanced English, third period Reading, fourth period P.E., fifth period Science, and sixth period Choir. Before I went to fifth period, the only class I had with any black girls was 3rd period. And in that class were three girls from Jodie McClure and the enemy Mr. Taylor's fifth grade class: Cheryl Pearson, Lelia Mills, and Estella Jones. So going into fifth period, I hadn't met anyone (female) different. No, I didn't care that much; I just wanted to make it through the day alive. When I went to Science, I sat down in one of the desks way in the back of the room and waited for the teacher to call the roll.

"Hey," a deep-sounding voice resonated behind me. I turned around expecting to see a boy, but it was a girl! And it was a nice-looking one at that. Her voice was way deeper than mine at that time. I still sounded like Mr. Bill.

"What's your name?" she asked.

"My name is Cedric," I replied trying not to sound in awe or like a squeaky mouse.

"My name is Velecia. Do you think this class will be hard?"

"Hmm, I hope not," I said. Thus the first <u>new</u> friend I would make at Judson would be in my fifth period class, a girl, and a girl with a voice deeper than mine. Her name was Velecia Stanton.

The second new friend I would make in the 6th grade was in my 6th period class. His name was Ray Ross. We just happened to be sitting next to each other in class and would wind up carrying on plenty of conversations. He told me he remembered me from East Ward. We were in different first and second grade classrooms back then, so I didn't really recall talking to him. But we were making up for it in this class. We talked a lot at the beginning of the school year. In fact, so much so that the teacher, Miss McFarland, tried to separate us by having Ray switch places with another boy who was talking a lot to his friend next to him. The result? Ray and the boy's friend named Bryant Roberts would do plenty of talking in class, while the boy who switched places with Ray would become one of my best friends through all three years at Judson. His name was Tony Mack.

Speaking of best friends, everybody asked, "How did you and Devin become such good friends?" Well, once upon a time, there was a boy who loved football and loved to play football or anything close to it. You know the boy. He's the author of this book. Anyway, remember the toss-up games I mentioned earlier? There would be a group of guys playing the games, and during these games, friendships were formed and/or destroyed and enemies were made and/or lost. And there was plenty of respect to be gained. If you were fast, had speed, moves, and could run and score touchdowns, you would gain respect. Back then, I learned who was fast, who had speed, who had moves, and who had power. Cleve Loyd, for example, had speed and power. He was already a legend in the elementary school city league. I will never forget the time he plain ran over me. He was coming right at me and boom, he ran me over like he was Earl Campbell. All I got was a piece of his shirt and a taste of the ground. And I *apologized* to him for tearing his shirt. Ha ha. Ray Stranger also had speed.

My good friend Tony was super fast. We always bragged about who was the fastest out of us. I'll admit it now: he was faster. Joseph Johnson had speed and power, also. Donny Morris was fast. Brion Van and Ray Ross had moves and quickness. Randolph Poole was fast. Charles Temple was fast and mean. Then, there was myself. Everybody said I was fast. Why? Because the first time we played, which might have been around the second or third day of school, I nearly caught Ray Stranger from behind after he broke one, and he already had a reputation for being one of the fastest guys in school, so that put me in that group. I proved myself by breaking long runs and scoring more often than not and catching slower people from behind (and sometimes faster people). During these games, you made friends, and Devin and I became friends while playing toss-up one day. I called him Dee back then, and I had the pleasure of running past him one time around end and scoring, then turning around later on and outrunning him on a long run for a touchdown. (Hey Devin, I'm sorry about that, but I was faster than you back then. Emphasis on "back then." OK? Are you happy?) He got me back one time when we all were playing tackle toss-up in a field adjacent to Judson's football field and, after I had broken several tackles, he nailed me from behind and drove me into the ground like a spike. As I recall, not too many guys were happy about that over-zealous tackle but I didn't say anything but "good tackle" to him and kept playing. Our friendship started right on the concrete of JMS and has continued ever since.

Two memories that stand out about Devin back in the salad days were the time he got into a fight with Ted Buckner at school and the time he came over to my house to play basketball on my new goal. I can remember the first time he came over to my house to play basketball because I was surprised that he had walked way over from his neighborhood to mine to come play ball. Today that doesn't seem like so much of a big distance, really, it might not be even a mile. But back then, to us little kids (and me being the littlest), it was like walking from Hallsville to Longview. Heck, the backyard felt like *a football field* with *eight of us* boys playing! I can remember the fight he had with Ted like it was yesterday because Devin very seldom got angry and was about as quiet as me, which was probably why we were such good friends. And it was shocking to see him react violently like that. Again, it was while we were playing a football game, and Devin tackled Ted like he was Jack Tatum or Ronnie Lott or somebody like that, and just planted him like yesterday's garden. (Devin loved to hit people, as one can tell.)Ted didn't like it and they started fighting. Devin tried to walk away, but Ted being Ted didn't think that was the end of it, and next thing you knew, they were rolling on the ground. That about covered it, I guess. Devin had one more fight later, and by then, *everyone* learned it was not smart to miss with him. He never got into another fight again. I wish I could've said the same thing for myself.

As for yours truly, that was a different story. The first fight I had in the sixth grade was with a friend and someone I had went to Jodie McClure with: Ron Lane. How did this happen? Well, it all started during P.E. when the coach was in a bad mood and decided to make us guys sit and watch the girls' P.E. class do gymnastics. And if any of us talked or made any kind of sound, we would get a paddling and a demerit or two. (By the way, whatever happened to demerits and paddling anyhow? Maybe that's why the school system is in so much trouble now today, *but that's another story for another day.*) Anyway, guess who was the first person who got in trouble? Really, I couldn't help it. The fattest girl in the sixth grade got on what I guess were called the balance bars, tried to act graceful, and wound up falling on her butt. I did good to just snicker, as did half the other guys, but the coach caught me and motioned for me to come and sit down next to him. Suddenly, the fat girl falling down wasn't so funny anymore and I didn't care if we were watching a bunch of girls in their shorts look silly. Seriously, I didn't care from the get-go. I could've been doing something better than this, like cleaning out trash cans or something. The bottom line was: I was in big trouble and I knew it. It didn't help matters any that seven others would join me in lining up for our paddlings because all I knew was that *I* was getting one. Well, I took my paddling and punishment like a man, I mean, like a 11-year old boy, meaning I had to act and look like it didn't hurt me and especially not cry. But inside, I was very, very upset that it had happened and the worst part of the whole thing had **NOT** occurred yet: I was going to have to tell Momma. With her, I knew I was going to cry. And the thought of it made me sick, mad, and irritated. So one can just imagined how I felt when, on the bus going home, all Ron could talk about was my paddling: how I got paddled, how I looked getting paddled, how the paddle looked, and well, you get the picture. He could've talked about anything...roaches, blood, death, anything but that, and it would not have bothered me. But all he wanted to talk about my paddling as if it were the funniest thing he'd seen in the last ten years. George, Bobby Jefferson, and Will Thomassen were having such a good time listening to Ron that I decided to join in the fun. I pulled Ron, who was seated in the seat in front of me, *over* the seat and started punching him in the eye. I was that angry. The fight ended as quickly as it started, as kids pulled us apart. We were still talking noise, however, and we continued doing so even as I got off the bus in front of my house. Momma heard me and actually already knew what had happened to me at school. I guess somebody must have called her, the coach or probably the principal, who knew Momma. And now the fight on the bus was the dang icing on the proverbial cake. We later went to Ron's house where I apologized rather reluctantly, and Ron and I basically forgot about the fight and continued being friends. And of course, I got fussed at and grounded.

Report Cards: 1979-1985

I was always under pressure to bring the best grades possible home (and so was just about everyone else I suppose) and usually, for some unknown reason or another, I always felt like I wasn't really doing that good. Yeah, my parents had a lot to do with that. If I made an 80, it should've been an 85. If I made a 90, it should've been a 95. If I made a 100, it should've been a 101. Seriously, if I made a 100, it should stay a

100, no matter what. Talk about asking for the impossible! And we're not going to go into grades below an 80 or below a 70…in those cases, we're talking groundings, whippings, stonings, etc.

Actually, I thought I did pretty good during the first semester of my final year. I had easy classes combined with tough classes, sort of half and half, so my report card usually wasn't too bad. The only class which really gave me problems was Calculus and I wound up with a 73 for the semester in that class. Other than that, everything else was either an A (Athletics and Office Aide) or B. (English, Economics, and Spanish) And though by this time I didn't actually care that much, I made the honor roll every six weeks that semester.

When I was in middle school, my parents were really hard on me to make the honor roll every time report cards came out, and for the most part, I succeeded. But they did not like for me or my sister to make C's or below on report cards, tests, homework, or anything else one could put a grade on. And if we did, we were asking for trouble. I can remember when I was in the seventh grade; I made a "C" in Advanced Math on my report card for the third six weeks. My average was about a 78 or 79, but on the report card, it showed "C." Today, they call these type of courses Pre-AP courses, but the way my parents reacted, you would've thought I'd failed every class I took that year. It didn't matter that I still made the honor roll even with the "C" (because it was an advanced course) and it didn't matter that because it was an advanced course, it was harder than the norm. No, all my parents saw was "C" as in "see" red and go ballistic. They grounded me, fussed at me, and basically all but excommunicated me from the normal world as I was not allowed to do anything close to fun for the next six weeks. I guess it helped because I made a "**D**" in the same class the next six weeks. Yeah.

Anyway, for the next few years up until my junior year in high school, even though I risked getting shot at by my parents (just kidding), I didn't care that much if I made the honor roll or not. I still made pretty good grades, but all I was concerned about was just doing good enough to keep from failing and keep from getting fussed at too much if I fell below my parents' (and my own) expectations. I still wanted "A"s and "B"s, but if I made a "C," it wasn't the end of the world. Like I said, I felt this way up until my junior year, and then I changed.

With everything else that year coming up roses, it shouldn't have been a surprise that my grades would be my best ever at LHS. I made the honor roll every six-weeks. Which shouldn't have been too hard to do since I was taking four advanced courses that year. But then again, I guess that's what made it such a great accomplishment. And I nearly made the school's national honor society but came up four points short of doing so. I had a 91 average compared to the 95 average one had to have to be considered. Still, I was proud of myself even if no one else was. In my parents' eyes, my grades unbelievably still weren't good enough to please them. I had a couple of "C"s that year, so they griped about those as well as wanting to see even higher grades. I started getting to the point (slowly but surely) where I had to tune them out at times. My teachers, my friends, and some of my friends' parents thought I did real good and looked at me like I was some sort of genius or something. Like, '*Wow, he sure is smart!*' But I've never looked at myself as being smart like some of the real brainy kids like Dave, Billy England, Kenneth Lewis, or Jocelyn Jones, to name a few.

They could make "A"s with their eyes closed. I guess maybe I could've done that, but I was happy with just being myself.

The Girl Who Tried to Kill Me: October, 1980

I have to tell this story about a particular classmate whom I will never forget, because Devin won't let me:

Back in the day, as in "when I used to go to Judson Middle School," a lot of us guys would play football usually in Judson's courtyard (if one could call it that; it was pure concrete) or out in one of the fields either before school, during lunch, or after school. Usually, it was touch football and quite naturally, usually it was only a bunch of us boys playing. But every now and then, we'd lose our minds and let a few girls play, and then we'd really go crazy and try to play tackle. The combination of girls, tackle football, and concrete was (and is) usually not a good and healthy mixture and during one particular spring day back in 1980, Rosetta Johnson would show me just how volatile a mixture that was.

I'm pretty sure y'all have heard the saying, "wrong place, wrong time." Well, this particular day was it for me. I was playing football with some of my other classmates, including Devin, who always seemed to be around when something was about to happen, and we decided to play tackle instead of touch football. Being the little seventh-grade idiots we were, it didn't matter to us if we were playing on a sidewalk or concrete (which we were) and it certainly didn't matter if we let two or three girls play with us including Tina Robbins and my friend, Rena Mack. Besides, we all were tough and the girls were bigger than half of us anyway. Myself, I was one of the shortest and smallest guys out there but also one of the fastest. Nobody was going to catch me and tackle me anyway if I did get the ball and break away, especially not some girl.

Then Rosetta entered the picture. She walked over and wanted to play and we let her. Who were we to argue? She was bigger and taller than all of us.

Not only was she bigger and taller, but she was definitely meaner. She might have even been faster since she did run track. Though we'd become better friends later on, I usually tried to stay out of her way back then. She was an athlete, not a sorry, petite, panty-waist kind of girl. She could probably beat half the boys back then in most sports. And really and truly, most of the girls at Judson were tough like that back then. But still and yet, I wasn't about to let no girl, tough or not, make a fool out of me. It just wasn't gonna happen.

Of course I was wrong. Dead wrong.

The first time I got the ball, I put on a move, ran to my right, and did a spin to avoid one of the guys. I never saw Rosetta coming. I was thinking "touchdown." It was a "touchdown" alright; Rosetta "touched" me and I went "down."

Really, I actually spun right into her arms as she caught me in mid-spin, bear-hugged me, picked me up, and planted me into the ground like a darn tree or something. The first thing that hit the ground was the back of my head. I lost the ball (no way I was going to hang on to the ball after *that* hit) and my senses. But then again, I probably had lost all my senses a few minutes before the hit when I agreed to take part in all this. Everybody went, "WOOOOOO!" and Rosetta stood over me, looked down at me and shouted, "Take that, *little boy*!" (I never forgot that part...I still hear that in some of my nightmares!) I got up and tried to act like I was alright but it was hopeless. If I had tried to talk, I would have probably gobbled like a turkey. I staggered away while all the rest of the guys either laughed or made fun of me and I practically collapsed onto one of the benches. I didn't play no more that day (or that month for that matter), and my head hurt me for weeks afterward. Devin, who was one of the hecklers, never forgot this embarrassment of mine, and thought it was the greatest hit he had ever seen. Rosetta would call me "little boy" for the rest of my life (actually for the next couple of years) and I would never play on concrete again. At least not until the next year, when I got tackled on some cement steps...

One more thing: R.J., if you happen to be reading this, that was a lucky tackle and that will never, ever happen again. (Smile)

Chasing the Pastor's Daughter: Summer 1982

On May 27, 1982, I started keeping a journal. That day ended the longest school year of my life, my 8th grade school year. Why was it so long? Because I was ready to leave Judson Middle School after three years of highs and lows (mostly lows) and ready to start a new (and hopefully, better) experience as a high school freshman. I wasn't the most popular person at Judson (unless one considers getting picked on popular, as I was in the 7th grade rather unmercifully at times) nor was I the most handsome person around. I was just an average 13-year old trying to make it through the beginning of my teen-age years with a sane and sound mind. I had a few close friends but was just about to start the "silent" period of my life as I was about to enter high school. I had a 10-year old sister who was about to be a 6th grader and who I wondered if she would be put through the same kind of misery I endured at Judson. I had parents who were strict with me while I was in middle school and if I didn't know what the word "strict" meant during that time, in the next few years I would certainly learn the meaning of the word.

The summer of 1982 was an interesting period of time for me because I was really going through some major physical and mental changes. Puberty was really kicking in and I was feeling it most definitely. Although I was still short and would be so when I started the first day of school in the 9th grade, everything else was changing-especially my voice and my..uh..hormones. When I was at Judson, I was in the school choir as a, get this, a second soprano, then became an alto in the 8th grade. Yes, my voice was that high. In fact, I made All-Region in the 8th grade as an alto, so obviously, I could sing back then. But during that summer, that changed drastically, as my voice dropped somewhere between Barry White and my granddaddy. It had gotten deep, deeper than Daddy's voice. I was sounding awful, trying to still talk high, but not really being able to and sounding like the poster child for puberty. Needless to say, my singing career was over. (It was going to be over anyway because I didn't want to sing in any choir anymore.)

The other thing that changed that summer was my hormones. Eversince Tangela had moved away before my 8th grade year started, my hormones had been left in neutral. I wasn't really interested in any girls that year, and although I was in a few clubs, I mainly kept to myself. The most interesting thing that happened to me in the 8th grade was my catching the chicken pox in April and having to miss two whole weeks of school. It was interesting because this was the starting point of my liking and chasing a girl who was younger than me for the next year or so. (Believe me; it was not as bad as it sounds.)

Back then, my momma, sister, and I attended St. John Baptist Church. And back then, there were a lot of kids and/or young people who attended church with us who were either around my age or my sister's age. They usually came with their parents to Sunday School, regular morning service, all or most of the various programs we had after church, and BTU. We all got along and going to church was a lot of fun back then. Our pastor was Rev. J.H. Hillsdale, and he was a strong leader as well as a nice person to us kids. Sis. Angela Hillsdale was his wife and they had two kids, Vanessa and Arnold. Sis. Hillsdale was over the youth, and we had a strong youth program with almost 100 kids there. My first experience with Sis. Hillsdale had occurred a couple of years earlier after my mom had joined church and was in the process of initiating us into the church's youth programs. Flower-child and I became ushers, sang in the youth choir, and took part in BTU, as well as Sunday School. It was about to be Christmas (you know where this is going) and Christmas in most churches meant Christmas plays and programs. Sis. Hillsdale had a play in mind and was passing out parts. She gave me the hardest part, playing the innkeeper who had no room for baby Jesus at his inn. (Yeah, I was just *thrilled* to get that part...) I was not very happy at first about having to play that part, but Sis. Hillsdale encouraged me and took away a lot of my fear, and I did very well in the Christmas program. (I did so well that in future Christmas and Easter plays we did, I always had one of the leading parts.)

Around this time, my sister and some of her friends had started giggling about something, but I had no idea what it was. A few weeks later, I found out. They came and told me that Vanessa liked me. Of course, Vanessa denied it ("No, I don't!!" she almost yelled), and I really didn't know how to react. Before that time, I really hadn't paid that much attention to her. However, that changed that particular Sunday. Although she said she didn't like me, she was never unfriendly towards me. When she had asked for my 8th grade picture and I gave it to her, I started to take notice. She was very pretty, had one of the nicest smiles I'd ever seen, and man, could she sing! I liked her instantly. I wanted her to be my girlfriend. But there were two problems: She was my pastor's daughter and she was the same age as my sister. For some reason, none of that didn't stop me as I wrote her notes, called her up on the phone almost everyday, and tried to figure out ways to be close to her. Yes, my hormones were raging out-of-control for the first time-I hadn't been nowhere near this aggressive with Tangela. And I wasn't too shy around Vanessa like I had been with Tangela. Vanessa's parents never said anything, they were really nice to me at a time when other parents would've probably wanted me to disappear, or worse, die. But I think they knew that I really liked their daughter in a purely, clean way, and that I was going through a 13-year-old moment. The high point of my chasing Vanessa (who never consented to be my girlfriend by the way) occurred when we got to do the devotion together during one of our afternoon programs. I was excited and cheesing like I'd won a million dollars, and what I remember most about that afternoon was the smile on Vanessa's face also while we did the devotion. It was worth a million dollars in itself.

In the spring of 1982, Vanessa caught the chicken pox. Two weeks later, I caught the chicken pox. I had it for two weeks and missed out on all kinds of activities at the time, but in a stupid and weird way, it felt good I had caught something from her. I would chase her throughout the summer of '82 (and part of '83 as well) until her family left St. John and moved to another church. (Yeah, it was kinda similar to what happened with Tangela.) It really broke my heart to see her and her family leave, and I was probably depressed for months afterward. (That's when I really entered my silent phase.) Things would not be the same at church for a long time, and I wouldn't try talking to another girl until the last part of my 10th grade year. Vanessa had been the one, and although she was younger than me, she was very mature for her age and I really respected and admired her a lot. Like? I liked her more than she knew.

J.T. Walton Introduces Me to Wrestling: May, 1983

When I was in the ninth grade, I met this guy named J.T. Walton. Hewas in my P.E. class and we became friends because usually we were on the same basketball, kickball, or baseball teams. As teammates, we meshed pretty well together. (And of course, if we were on opposing teams, we would usually try to kill one another.) We talked and tripped out about a lot of different things and besides Dave and Devin, he may have been the only other person I talked to on a regular basis during the ninth and tenth grade years. Remember, those were the two years I was a recluse in and out of school. He came by the house to visit and play basketball a few times even though he lived a dozen or more blocks away. Not only would we play basketball at my house, he lived close to a park which had basketball goals, and I would ride my bike to his house and we would go play basketball at that park. Somehow we didn't see one another all that much when we became juniors and seniors, but we stayed friends despite that. I won't ever forget we were the ping-pong champions of the world, or at least, of our class. We beat every other team in the class, and I don't recall us losing to anyone. We called ourselves, "Domination Incorporated."

The name of our little team ironically came from one of J.T.'s favorite pastimes. I had heard many kids and some of my friend's mention that they watched pro wrestling on Saturdays but I had never done so. Every Monday, J.T. would tell me about what he saw happen on either *Mid-South Wrestling* or *World Class Championship Wrestling* and he made it sound like they were the most exciting programs to watch bar none. I had last watched wrestling when I was five years old and I really didn't like it back then. To be honest, it sort of scared me. (No, I don't know why.) Now I had been hearing about *the Junkyard Dog, Ted Dibasse, the Von Erichs, Chris Adams, Butch Reed, Iceman Parsons, Terry Taylor,* and *the Freebirds*, to name a few, on a regular basis and it sounded pretty interesting. J.T. was really into it and he'd tell me to watch the shows when they came on T.V. I wasn't doing much of anything else, so one Saturday afternoon I convinced my sister to watch *Mid-South Wrestling* with me, and after we saw it for the first time, we were hooked like catfish. If nothing else, Saturdays became *Mid-South Wrestling.*

We had to watch it, no matter what. If we were outside playing or doing some work or something, when wrestling came on, we stopped what we were doing and ran to the nearest TV. (If we happened to be doing chores, we did them faster.) If we weren't at home and had gone out-of-town, we suffered. We didn't have VCRs back then, so if we missed a program, it was missed for good, unless they showed last week's highlights the very next Saturday. It really got to be something else. We scheduled our Saturdays around all the wrestling shows: 11 a.m.-*World Class Championship Wrestling* on Channel 6, 1 p.m.-*Mid-South Wrestling* on Ch. 3, and 10 p.m.-*Championship Sports Wrestling* on Ch. 11 (if I could get away with staying up to see it). We watched them (especially Mid-south) every Saturday and it got to the point where if a show wasn't too good (for example, a show where all the good guys lost, got jumped on and beat up, or humiliated in some kind of diabolical way), then our Saturday was screwed up. Our heroes were the one and only *Junkyard Dog* (who probably everyone this side of the Mississippi loved), *Hacksaw Duggan, Butch Reed,* all of the *Von Erichs, Terry Taylor, Iceman Parsons,* and *Chris Adams,* who was J.T.'s favorite. Some of the wrestlers we couldn't stand included *Ted Dibasse* (my least favorite wrestler at the time), the *Freebirds, the Midnight Express* and their irritating manager *Jim Cornette, King Kong Bundy,* and *Skandor Akbar's Devastation Incorporated,* the name which served as the inspiration behind my and J.T.'s team name. Many times, the good guys won the belts or beat up on the villains, and we were happy. Sometimes, however, the bad guys would win (usually by cheating) or they'd have their way with the good guys and it would get kind of ugly at times. When that happened, my sister and I would usually turn off the TV and go outside and dig holes in the ground. In fact, the whole neighborhood would turn into a wake. Everybody watched wrestling back then. However, come Monday, good or bad, J.T.

and I would discuss the past Saturday's events as if we were a couple of those sports analysts or commentators and try to figure out or predict (or hope) what would happen next Saturday.

For the next few years, we had good Saturdays and we had BAD Saturdays. I had to cut down on watching wrestling during my senior year due to more important things, such as my nerves and health; I didn't want to have a heart attack behind all this. My sister had outright stopped watching wrestling the year before when it seemed there were almost too many bad Saturdays. I still watched it every now and then and it still was kind of exciting, but as times changed, people, places, and things changed, including myself and pro wrestling itself. The wrestling programs we grew up with were cancelled, some of the wrestlers retired or passed away, and it just wasn't the same. Every now and then, I watch wrestling in its current form, but it's just not Mid-south Wrestling anymore, and I miss it.

The Legend of Big B.: April-May, 1984

As early as my freshman year in school, I had heard about the legend of "Big B." Some examples: *'Big B. beat up this dude yesterday...with one hand!'* Or: *'Big B. whipped this boy in class a week ago, then beat up his brother this week.'* Or how about this one: *'Big B. took on a whole family yesterday, and won!'*

Big B. was either the toughest and meanest dude in the southern part of the United States, or the ugliest, nastiest, and scariest person you'd ever meet. Or maybe both. At the time, I didn't know. All I knew was that I did not want to run into this person on a bad day or on a good day. In fact, I didn't want to run into Big B. on any day, period. The kids made Big B.

sound like he was one step away from the crazy house, or state pen, or both. Not only would he snap his own mind, but he'd probably snap necks, arms, and legs as well. I had imagined him to be 6'9" and 300 pounds, with arms like tree trunks, and fists that could break up bricks. Big B. probably ate wild animals for dinner with rusty nails as in appetizer, and washed it all down with acid. And if that didn't make a person mean, then nothing would.

So for almost three years, the stories and beatings continued from a distance. I had been fortunate not to have run into this certain candidate for "Most Likely to go to Jail in the Future" during that time, but then one day my momma came home and gave my sister and me some distressing news:

"We are going to have company this weekend and Monday."

"Who?"

"She goes to LHS with you, Cedric. She's had a rough time with school."

"Who is she?" Flower asked.

"Her name is Beverly, but her friends call her Big B."

I did a double-take and looked at Flower, who looked stricken, surprised, and sick, all at one time. "Say what?" she said, "D-Did you say, Big B.?" The terror was beginning to grow inside my sister and me.

"Yes. I heard she stays in trouble at school, and at home, her situation is not the best of situations. She really needed someone to talk to and listen to her. I've had her in my classes, and she's a sweet person once you get to know her."

My momma seemed convinced of what she was saying. Myself, I was somewhere in between shock and fear. I was thinking two things: *Big B. is a GIRL???* (Considering how Rosetta had nearly knocked me out in middle school, that was probably *worse*), and, *Is Momma out of her mind for inviting this crazy person to our house??* Flower-child had a somewhat better grasp of the situation, and she expressed herself thusly: "Momma, Big B. EATS people!!" Momma just looked at her and said, "Big B. will knock you out if you even breathe around her! She's meaner than...than...the devil!!"

"Nonsense," said Momma. "She's just had a rough time is all. Really, she's friendly once you get to know her." I was trying to take all of this in and having a hard time doing so, and I tried to think of something I had to do that day when Big B. came to visit, something important. Like, for example, live. "She really is a nice, young lady." Flower-child and I looked at each other and rolled our eyes as if to say, *Yeah, right. We are in big trouble.*

And so it came to pass one Sunday morning, before we went to church, that Momma went to go pick up the dreaded "Big B." Flower and I rode shotgun. (Well, we felt we were going to need one, at least.) We drove up to Big B.'s house, which miraculously was a house, and not some cave, and as the front door opened, Flower looked at me and said, "Well, Brother, it's been nice knowing you." I was about to answer until someone stepped onto the front porch and walked towards our car. Someone very attractive, tall, and definitely fine. She got into the car and said hello, then

Momma spoke: "Cedric, Flower, this is Beverly. Beverly, these are my two kids, Cedric and Flower." Flower said hello and tried to get my attention, but my attention was on Big B., er, I mean, Beverly. She had long, curly hair, a pretty face, and was built perfectly. The song, *Brickhouse*, played in my head, because it fit her perfectly. Flower, after awhile, finally got my attention. "This CAN'T be Big B.!" She whispered, looking at Beverly. "No way," I said, "but if it is, she can beat me up anytime." Flower groaned and shook her head, "Just like a boy. Always losing his mind over some girl."

"SO," I said, focusing on Beverly, "You go to LHS? Are you a freshman or sophomore?"

"I'm a freshman."

"You sure are," I thought to myself. We continued talking to her the rest of the day (I even sat next to her during church, admiring her better qualities) and really had a pretty good time. I forgot almost totally that this was the Big B. everybody and their mommas feared. She admitted to me that she was indeed the infamous Big B. and that most (but not all) of the stories were true, and we actually laughed and joked about them. Not too surprisingly, I rather enjoyed her company. The next day, which happened to be a holiday, we picked her up, and she spent the day with us again. As I'd said, she was tall, a little taller than myself, so we went outside and played basketball. We played two or three games against each other, and that was fun, in more ways than one if you know what I mean. In fact, the basketball games and the "physical" nature of the games might have prompted the small speech my momma gave me after she took Beverly

home.

"Cedric, remember that you are not to be trying to make her your girlfriend or something. She is to be like family, like having another little sister."

"Great," I thought, *"just what I needed. Another 'little' sister."*

"Do you understand? I better not catch you talking to her out the way or trying to be her boyfriend. If I do, I'm going to whup your behind. Got it?"

"I've got it," I said, wondering if I'd ever have a girlfriend. As long as

Momma was around, it didn't look like it. I went to my room, and as I passed Flower's room, she poked her head out the door and said, "You can't win for losing, can you, brother?"

No, I can't...

Now it was 1986, and things still hadn't changed. I knew my parents (especially my momma) looked at me and all they saw was their little boy, but I wasn't little no more, nor was I a kid. I was 17 years old and trying to be grown. I wasn't trying to be disrespectful or anything, but I was just acting my age (unfortunately). And what was it people say about too many grown people being in one house? I thought on all this and finally went to sleep.

CHAPTER 11

The Birth of the House Rockers

Friday, January 10, 1986

When school was out, I went to go visit Dave, who talked me into going back home and trying to work things out with my parents. I didn't tell them I was going to see Dave, so they had no idea where I was, unless Flower told them. It was not like me to not let them know where I was going, if they let me go. So they probably figured, *"Wow, he is really angry."* I was gone only a couple of hours at the most. Leaving home wouldn't have solved anything anyway. Nobody said anything to me when I came back home. (Correction: My sister spoke to me. She said, "Welcome back, dummy.") I didn't get fussed at or anything like that. Daddy might have said something along the lines of letting them know something if I was going to go visiting without coming home first, but other than that, nothing else was said. Momma didn't say anything period, and I never had any other problems along those lines again. (Well, not for a year or two, at least.) My momma, sister, and I went to go visit our neighbors. Then a little later after we went back home, Devin came over and beat me five games straight in basketball.

My parents never said anything else about what happened.

I wanted to forget about it.

Devin said I should run away more often.

Things were back to normal.

The Origin of the House Rockers

Friday, January 17

The third week of the year would be just as memorable and crazy as the first couple of weeks. The second week would see the formation of the greatest tag-team in dominoes history. Well, maybe not THE greatest but a pretty darn good team nonetheless. We are talking about "Loverboy" Devin M. and "Sweet" Ced E., the one and only HOUSE ROCKERS! This incredible week would also spawn the feared "Round Table". We'll be hearing more about them in a later chapter. Right now, it's time for the...<u>Origin of the House Rockers!</u>

Our humble beginnings took place one cold and clear day during 4th period Athletics after the football season had ended. With the season being over and there being no more practices, at least no more for us seniors, we would basically all meet in the field house and do whatever we felt like or needed to be doing. Some of us would read, study, or do homework. Most of us would shoot the breeze, take a nap, trip out, or horse around. Then some of us would play dominoes, usually doubles, which was two-on-two. Back then, there were some wars and some pretty tough customers--Andre Morris and Theo Friday, Harold Loyd and Tony Simmons, Freddy Woods and Tank Thomas, and possibly the toughest of the tough, Jonathan Cobb and Kenneth Avery. They were the acknowledged champions. They could beat you and make you like it. They knew exactly what they were doing in that they could set you up and make you play what they wanted you to play, and usually what they wanted, they usually got. Before you knew it, you and your partner would be getting up after getting your tails handed to you on a stick.

This day, after another grueling session of Mr. Polawski's Economics

Torture Class, Devin and I headed for the field house discussing our favorite subject.

"What's up between you and Annette?" Devin wanted to know.

"I don't know. I can't tell whether she likes me, hates me, or somewhere in between. You and Valecia still talking?"

Devin replied, "Yeah, but that's up and down, too. I can't see why you and Annette can't get together. I think she likes you."

"You always say that. Anyway, I can't tell." I replied. "Not half the time, anyway."

As we went through the gym and headed for the steps leading down to the field house, we passed this girl named Shelia Rhodes and one of her friends talking to each other. Shelia was a tenth-grader who lived in my neighborhood and rode my bus. I didn't know her very well, but I knew she went with one of my classmates. Little did I know that I was about to get real acquainted with Shelia later on before the day ended and in a surprising way at that. In fact, little did I know that I was about to get acquainted and re-acquainted with a lot of girls that week.

But right now, it was Monday, and as Devin and I entered the field house, we passed Jon and Kenneth giving yet another painful lesson to some hapless opponents. After the coaches took roll and after we couldn't find anything else better to do, we decided to look in on the dominoes battle taking place.

"Look at that," I told Devin.

Jon and Kenneth were looking unbeatable, and that day, it was obvious that they were on a higher level than anybody else. "Get up!" Kenneth shouted as they won yet another game. "Nobody can beat us! Who's next?" Jon wanted to know. When it looked like no one was going to be brave enough to sit down against the two juggernauts, Jon exclaimed, "We are the champions! No one can hang with us! No one can stop us!" When Kenneth reiterated more of the same including begging somebody to sit down and take a butt-whipping, I couldn't take it anymore. Something inside of me snapped.

"Devin, you want to play?" I asked. "I think we can take them."

Devin looked at me as if I had lost my mind.

"I don't know how to play dominoes that well. Do you?" he asked.

"Yeah, I play all the time." Actually, my dominoes playing up to that point had consisted of being beaten by my momma and Mr. Queen on a regular basis. Despite all that, however, I felt strangely confident.

"C'mon Devin. Might as well try. They can't be *that* good."

"Well, alright." Devin did not sound very confident.

At first, Kenneth and Jon looked at us as if they couldn't believe that Devin and I, obviously real amateurs in their eyes, would have the nerve to sit down at *their* table in *their* sport and face them at *their* game. Their disbelief then turned to joy, however, as it turned into the kind of joy hunters have when they're about to pounce upon some peg-legged deer. In this case, guess who were the deer? There was no doubt about it--we were doomed.

Or so everybody thought.

I told Devin that if I got the down, then all I wanted him to do was count. I didn't care if it was but five, take it. I may have been only an average player at the time, but I knew how to keep a down, set my partner up, and play some defense. My granddaddy had been a GREAT and FEARED dominoes player; he had won all sorts of trophies in the past, so I guess I was beginning to inherit his genes in that direction. Also, I knew what to do if I had a great hand (for example, holding almost all of the fives) and how to use it against my opponents. And for some reason, on this day, I had a great hand every hand. With Devin and me counting, myself keeping the down, and basically not letting Kenneth and Jon run wild, we kept it close until the final hand. We needed five points to win, and they needed ten. It was my play. I couldn't count anything so I had to "roll" Jon over to my partner by making him play something Devin could count off. Devin was already doing a very good job of counting for someone who claimed had not ever played dominoes before, so it wasn't hard. Jon, obviously angry, ("*#$*! I don't believe this!" he screamed) and who couldn't count even if his life depended on it, played what I wanted him to play, and Devin scored the winning points off his play.

"Dime-time! (10 points) That's game!" Devin shouted.

By this time, a crowd had gathered around, mostly those who had lost to Kenneth and Jon in the past, and when they saw us defeat the two villains, they went crazy as if we had won the Super Bowl.

"Devin and Cedric are the new champions! You both lost!"

"How does it feel, LOSERS?"

"Y'all are sorry! First time they sit down and they beat y'all!"

"They're the greatest! They're the champions!" Well, maybe the guys didn't go that far, but we were recognized as the new champs.

Devin and I gave each other a high-five and sat back and basked in the adulation. Obviously, Kenneth and Jon weren't taking part in the adulation proceedings and they were absolutely P.O.'d. They didn't really believe we had actually won.

"We want a freakin' rematch!" Kenneth shouted.

"That was a FLUKE, pure and simple!" Jon practically bullhorned.

"C'mon, let's go at it again. No one else wants to sit down. What do you two lucky weaklings say?"

I looked around. No one else really wanted to play and everyone in the room wanted to see us go at it again. I looked at Devin. He was looking like we ought to get while the getting was good. But deep down, he, like myself, wanted to legitimize our victory by beating them again, so he gave me the "high" sign. "Let's do this," Devin said. "Let's go. Shake 'em up." I was ready and Devin looked and sounded a little more confident this time.

The rematch was worse...for Jon and Kenneth. This time it seemed that every hand I pulled had at least five 5s in it. Jon and Kenneth didn't look like they were pulling much of anything, and Devin knew all he had to do was count and get out of the way because as I so eloquently put it during the bashing, "I'm running the show, brothers. This is MY beat." And Kenneth and Jon knew it. They also knew there wasn't anything they could do about it. Devin almost didn't have to count, much less play. After a barrage of tens, fifteens, twenties, and even a thirty-count or two, it was all over but the crying. (Or the laughter depending on whose side you were on.) Final: House Rockers 150, Former Champions 60. No doubt about it: Greatness was born that day.

After Jon and Kenneth got up, shook our hands, and admitted we were great (Actually, they got up, cursed a little, and just shook their heads in disbelief), Devin and I left and headed for lunch.

"Man, I had no idea what I was doing," Devin said, "I was just matching dots and taking counts when I could. I'm glad you had the real good hands because you knew what you were doing."

"You did real good," I told him, "I did have an idea of what I was doing, but those hands I was pulling were incredible! I didn't have to do much except take it to them with those fives."

"You said it, little man. Jon and Kenneth weren't really prepared for that and they had it kind of easy before we sat down."

"*Had* is the key word, brother. Now we're the champions."

"*And it feels good,*" sang Devin as we laughed our way into the cafeteria.

The next day Jon and Kenneth were waiting for us at the entrance. Of course, once again, they wanted a rematch. Once again, they said we were flukes. Once again, they knew they could overpower us. Once again, they got their heads handed to them on a stick by the magnificent team of Devin M. and Cedric E.

This time we almost couldn't believe it ourselves. For weeks, Jon and Kenneth had been beating everybody in the place; now, all of a sudden, they couldn't beat two guys who shouldn't have been in their league. In fact, suddenly, nobody could beat us the next few days. That week--the last week before the schedule changes began to take place to mark the beginning of the second semester--we were unstoppable. Eight games, eight wins. We were undefeated by the end of the week. We would leave 4th period Athletics the undisputed domino champions.

CHAPTER 12

The Round Table

Thursday, January 16, 1986

While all this winning was going on, I continued trying to figure out where I stood with Annette. Like I said, some days it seemed like we were destined to go together in some form or fashion; and some days it seemed like we didn't know one another. Longview High School's Senior Celebration was fast approaching, and she and one other girl (Guess who?) had been the only girls I had even considered asking to be their escort and date. I wasn't in any hurry; I didn't really consider going to the Senior Celebration all that important. Deep down, I wanted to go, but I didn't (A) want to make a fool out of myself, (B) want to just escort anyone, (C) want to make a fool out of myself (D) want to figure out a way to take myself and some girl out on a date afterwards, and most importantly, (E) want to make a total fool out of myself, which in that type of environment would've been real easy to do. Seeing how the risks outweighed the benefits, real or imagined, I didn't worry about it too much.

Besides, I was now one-half of the undisputed tag-team domino champions of the world! Well, maybe not the real world, but LHS was my world. I was thinking about that and its ramifications (today the field house, tomorrow money-making tournaments!) as I got on the bus to go home and sat next to Big Louis. He spoke and I said, "What's up?", and after a few minutes of idle chatter, I stared out the window thinking about how there should be a National Dominoes League or something.

As I thought about the looks on Jon's and Kenneth's faces after we beat them the second time, all of a sudden I felt a hand slide across my chest as if to rub it. My first thought was, *"What the hell...?"* Then I heard a feminine voice attached to the hand: "He sure is cute and he knows I like him." Huh?? I turned around and looked behind me from whence the hand actually came from and looked straight into the eyes of Shelia Rhodes. (Remember her from the previous chapter?) She had broken up quite publicly with one of my friends only last week, and suddenly it was very obvious she was over him. She and her audience of Meesha Drew and Sonya Jace, a couple of my sister's friends and two of Shelia's sophomore contemporaries, were seemingly having a good time at my expense, and with my tongue tied up in a square knot in my mouth, she continued: "I think he is so fine. I really want to get with him and..." And so forth and so on as her friends giggled themselves silly. Louis said, "Do you hear that? She wants you. You ought to go after that." I mumbled something like, "Yeah, right." as I glanced around trying to figure out where Flower-child was sitting, because if she was seeing and hearing this, she could blackmail me until the cows came home. Fortunately, Flower was sitting way up front looking straight ahead, so she had no idea what her friends were doing and what was happening. Then I figured, *Well, Shelia is having her little joke. She's not being serious.* So I basically ignored her and her little friends the rest of the trek home. They were all in the 10th grade at the time and thought they were grown. When the bus reached my stop and I got up to get off the bus, she pinched me in the behind and sensually told me bye. I forgot all about dominoes right then and there.

The next day, as Devin and I headed for the field house, we took a shortcut and cut through the gym. Like a bad dream, there was Shelia again standing by the steps talking to a friend. *"Oh no,"* I thought to myself and knew what was coming.

"Hi Baby," she said, "me and you have got to get together someday."

And she pinched me in the butt again. I almost ran down the steps to get away. Devin was like, "Whoa, Ced! What is this? Did I just hear what I thought I heard?"

I told him sarcastically and nervously, "No, that was just your imagination. Besides, she ain't being serious, she's just goofing around."

"Well, sounds like to me she wants to "goof around" with you."

"Why would I want to talk to her for, anyway? She just broke up with Bobby last week and she's not my type anyway."

"What *is* your type? You know you shouldn't turn down a free meal when it's presented to you like this. I know I wouldn't."

"Oh, really?" I said, thinking Devin would've probably ran faster from her than I would.

"Come on, she's not serious, Devin. I'm telling you, this is all a big joke." I was trying to convince myself that it was and saying it made it seem it was. Shelia really wasn't bad-looking at all, she was kinda cute. But I never try to go with any of my classmates' ex-girlfriends. It just wasn't something I'd do. And I really felt she really wasn't being serious anyway.

"Whatever you say. But remember, you're the Don Juan of the class of

1986! Ha Ha Ha," laughed Devin. I tuned him out.

I was trying to put Shelia out of my mind and Devin wasn't helping. But after we had entered the field house and had taken care of Jon and Kenneth once again, the only thing on my mind was how great the present (and future) House Rockers were. But within the space of half an hour, all that would change as I would forget about dominoes and Shelia for the next two to three hours…

After leaving the fieldhouse, Devin and I decided to go to lunch. We walked into the cafeteria champions; A few minutes later, we would run out of it broken-down fools. As usual, it was my fault. The cafeteria was noticeably crowded and students were getting their food and having a hard time finding somewhere to sit. And so it was with Devin and me. We walked around trying to find a seat but couldn't find one, so we decided to split up and look. Lo and behold, I spotted Wendy sitting at a table all by herself. I asked her was anyone else sitting there, she told me no, and so I left my tray at the table to go find Devin. Which I did. But to paraphrase a popular *Fatboys* song back in the day, when we went back to the table, what did we see? The eyes of <u>SIX</u> girls staring back at me (and Devin)! Devin was like, "I <u>*know*</u> we're not fixing to sit there."

I thought to myself, *"And this coming from a man who said he doesn't turn down free meals."* Then I looked again and thought, *" He's right! It would be a huge mistake to sit with these girls."*

I actually wanted to take off running and leave my tray at that table. I'm not ashamed to admit I wasn't feeling brave right at that particular moment. Not with six girls looking at us as if Thanksgiving dinner had arrived. At the table besides Wendy now sat Robrina Houston, Diana

London, Joyce Melrose, Chandra Smith, and (shudder) Traci! Wendy was usually down-to-earth and alright, but when she and Joyce got together, it was usually mayhem. You add Robrina, who I'd known since the 6th grade and who had always been a pretty good friend, to the mix and you've got trouble. I didn't know Diana or Chandra too well (yet), but I had heard different things, not all of it good. And Traci, well, was still Traci. Just looking at her made me weak.

"Hey! Come sit down! Where are y'all going? We won't bite! Come sit with us!" I had no idea that Joyce, Wendy, and Robrina could be so loud. They were actually louder than a cafeteria full of people. Maybe louder than a sold-out Texas Stadium. I looked around to make sure Flower was nowhere around to see this. We had the same lunch period unfortunately. They made Devin sit next to Traci (the lucky guy!) and I had to sit in between Wendy and Joyce, which wouldn't have been any worse than sitting in the electric chair at midnight. What followed was as savage a grilling as might be found at all the bar-b-q establishments in Longview combined.

"Look at Devin over there being so quiet. He's not fooling us. We know he's a stud, ain't that right, De-vin?" Joyce was just getting warmed up.

Devin looked like a condemned man walking the last mile.

"And you, Cedric, you don't fool us either." I jumped as Robrina turned on me with a vengeance. "We know you used to have it bad for Traci. We read some of those notes you wrote to her. Remember those notes?" Robrina and Traci looked at one another and smiled.

I probably turned a different shade of color not discovered yet. I wanted to die.

They continued: (Especially Joyce, who got louder by the second.)

"Devin, how many girlfriends have you had?"

"Look at him. He probably wants to add Traci to the list."

"Or probably Chandra."

"Do you think we're cute, De-vin? Are we fine?"

"What about you, Cedric? Do we look good to you?"

"What kind of women do you prefer anyway? The ones with <censored> or the ones with <ditto>?" (*They actually said the real words!*)

"Bet you want to kiss one of us, don't you?"

"And I bet we can guess which ONE! HA HA HA!"

"*Can* you or Devin kiss?"

"Now that football season is over, y'all will have more time for us girls."

"What's the matter, Devin? Cat got your tongue?"

"Boy, Cedric sure is sweating. Do you sweat like that when you're..."

OKAY, needless to say, at that moment, being with Shelia or even Randressa in a small, locked closet would've probably been better than sitting at the table with these hyenas. Devin looked as if he had died a thousand deaths and as if he wanted to share some of those deaths with me for putting him in this position. Myself, it was a combination of the shock at how loud Joyce, who was really relentless in the attack, could get, and the anxiety of sitting only a foot away from Traci, who probably could've and would've made me do things that were against the law. My fork felt like it weighed 500 pounds and the food had no taste to it. My fish basket looked like roadkill. Really, it was time to go. It had <u>been</u> time to go. I looked at Devin and boldly said, "We've got to go." Then Joyce asked us, "Are y'all going to take our trays for us?"

I looked at Devin. Devin came to life and answered, "Heck, no! If anything, y'all are going to carry <u>our</u> trays back. Let's go, Ced E."

And with that, we took off walking real fast and left our trays with them! Joyce and Wendy nearly had a fit and started screaming for Mrs. Reeves, the assistant principal, who was in the middle of the cafeteria. When we heard that, we took off like a shot and didn't stop running until we reached our lockers, laughing all the way there.

The following Thursday after school, I went out to eat with my mom and my sister at the Butcher Shop. While my mom went off to talk to a friend, my sister and I sat looking out a window. Suddenly, I heard some disturbingly familiar voices calling my name.

"Cedric! Oh, CEDRIC!"

I didn't really want to look but I did anyway, and there was Wendy, Robrina, Diana, and Traci (again) enjoying dinner. "Come here," they said. I looked at Flower, who smiled as if she had struck gold, and hesitantly got up. "Get over there and show 'em you're the man," Flower said, snickering, "better hurry up before Momma gets back."

"Dang," I muttered to myself.

I walked over there expecting more of what I got the last time I was around them, but this time they acted civilly towards me. I guess it was because Joyce wasn't around. I talked to them and tried not to look at Traci too hard or too much, which wasn't easy. They told me they missed me sitting with them in the cafeteria. I thought, *"Yeah, sure y'all did. Y'all missed making me nervous with all that crazy talk."* But I told them that someday I'll come back and sit with them one day, but it wouldn't be soon. I must've been out-of-my-mind to have said that.

I went back to Flower who viewed all this quite intently, and then when they got ready to leave, they told me they'd see me later, hopefully in the cafeteria at school the next day. Traci told me bye in her sexy voice again. Obviously she took delight in telling me bye and looking at me slobber like a baby. They left before we ate so I was able to have somewhat of an appetite.

"You're the man," Flower-child said.

"Oh, shut up."

Next day:

"You told them WHAT?" Devin looked at me as if I'd lost it.

"I told them I'd sit with them sometimes during lunch."

"You know what? That's a round table we sat at with those nuts, so I'm going to call them the "Round Table" from now on. Queen Joyce and her knights. And you're going to be the Court Jester." Devin shook his head and said, "You're just doing this so you can be close to Traci. Well, what about Annette? Better yet, what about Shelia?"

What about Annette? She hadn't talked to me in a while and with all this other stuff going on, I hadn't been thinking of her too much. Shelia? Well, after we left the Butcher Shop and went home, I found myself taking a walk through the neighborhood and I just happened to run into her. She only lived right around the corner from me anyway. We started talking to each other, and I was beginning to think that this girl was serious. She really wanted to get with me. We talked for about thirty minutes then I went on my way, all the while thinking, *Should I get with her? Should I talk to her?*

During the next couple of weeks, I tried to make up my mind about Shelia. She was cute and fine, but she was also kind of fast. Maybe too fast for me. She'd come by and visit a couple of times and I'd go visit her at her house and sometimes we'd go for a walk in the neighborhood, but I never felt we should go together. I just wasn't that serious about her. Of course, she told me all the different things she wanted to do to and with me, but I never really took her seriously. She tried, but it never happened. I just wouldn't let it.

Besides I had the Senior Celebration and the Prom to worry about within the next three months, and I already had an idea of who I wanted to go with to one of those events. And it sure wasn't no tenth grader.

CHAPTER 13

What is Calculus?

Monday, January 20, 1986

cal-cu-lus: *Math*. A method of calculating by the use of a highly specialized system of algebraic symbols.

Not even the definition made sense.

I don't know what made me decide to take Calculus my final year in school other than the fact I liked math and liked doing math problems. I've had tough math courses before (Geometry just about did me in back when I was in the ninth grade), but *this* took the cake, a*nd ice cream.* This was the hardest course to comprehend and figure out. I was in there a whole year and I never did understand what I was doing the entire time. And I guarantee you I wasn't the only one. There were students who took Calculus who were in the upper ten percent of our class who let this course eat them up alive. Not that they had any choice in the matter. There were only about forty of us taking the class spread over two periods and maybe a dozen of us actually knew what we were doing or were even mildly interested in the class. Mr. Crawford (we called him "Mr. Double C-- "Calculus Crawford") was our teacher, and he had been teaching high school math for almost 40 years at the time. He obviously *knew* what he was teaching, but some of us just couldn't see what he saw most of the time. Most of us were lost and *stayed* lost through the school year; a few of us didn't really care about the class (we only had one more semester to go anyway); and some of us were bored silly. Most of the time, I fell in with the "lost" group.

I knew I was in trouble the first time I brought some Calculus homework home and asked my parents for help and they looked at it and looked at it and looked at it, and finally went to bed without telling me anything. Another time, Daddy told me: "You're on your own, kid. Do the best you can with it, as long as you pass." This may have been the first time ever my parents said it was okay for me to make a "C" in a class. Seriously, though, they didn't understand Calculus any better than I did. One time, I had ten problems for homework. I started on the first problem at 6:00 p.m. and didn't finish it until 9:00 p.m. I said to myself, *Ok, that's enough.* Daddy came into my room and asked me whether or not I was finished with my homework, I said yes, and he asked to see it. I showed him my one problem which took up a whole sheet of paper, and he looked at it and said, "That's good."

I and the rest of my class were fortunate that Mr. Double C. graded homework on whether you attempted it or not (and not just scribbling down something, mind you; you really had to try to solve the problems) and not on how many you got right or wrong. If he had, everybody except for maybe three or four of us would've failed. At times, he graded the tests we took the same way, but most of the time he graded them outright. Like I mentioned before, one time he caught me trying to cheat, but he really didn't get on me too bad or discipline me in any way because the notes I were trying to use weren't doing me any good anyway. That was the *only* time in my life I ever tried to cheat on a test, so you can see I really wasn't good at it. And, my heart wasn't in it anyway.

I started off having Calculus fifth period, and then during the second semester after the schedule changes, I had it fourth period. Both times, however, it was boring and hard. At least Dave was in the fourth period version and we kept our streak intact of having a class together every year since we started high school. We had to keep each other awake, which wasn't easy. We'd be staring at the overhead projector screen as Double C droned on, and we would look at the numbers, letters, and symbols put into forms meant to confuse. If we didn't know any better, we would swear that was Chinese writing up there, ancient Chinese writing at that. A normal class day would go something like this...

Wednesday, January 22

Dave and I had entered our fourth period class expecting more of the usual. "The longest forty-five minutes of the day," I muttered.

"C'mon, it's not that bad."

"Easy for Dave to talk," I thought to myself, *"he could sleep the whole period and still know more than the entire class. The rest of us poor slobs had to try to stay awake in order to learn something."*

I sat down at my desk. Dave sat down behind me. Mr. Double C. started lecturing and drawing and writing all kinds of numbers, letters, symbols, and objects.

"Man, this class sure is boring," I started grumbling.

Dave poked me in the back to keep me from dozing off. I looked at my watch. Class was but five minutes gone. It felt like an hour.

He replied, "Yeah, it sure is. Only forty minutes to go until the bell.

Whoopie."

I looked around the class to see if anyone else was paying as much attention as we were. Four of them looked asleep, three of them *were* asleep, and five of them looked as bored as we did. "This is the dullest class I have ever had. How is this stuff going to help me when I get older? Everything's boring: the teacher, the book, the desks, the chalkboard, the chalk...everything!" I was miserable.

Dave started snoring.

"Wake up, Dave! Psst! Wake up!" I loudly whispered. I couldn't see him unless I turned around in my desk to look at him, but I sure could hear him. Double C continued his droning, "X *times the cosine of y equals...*" I looked at my watch again. Then I looked at the clock. Only eight minutes had passed. It felt more like a hundred. I felt like screaming. I was thinking, *I'd rather deal with ten Mr. Polawskis than this. At least he's not this boring.* Although it was also a difficult class, Economics was at least mildly interesting. Calculus was hard *and* boring...a devastating combination to say the least.

Dave woke up and asked, "Drawn anything good lately?"

For once, I hadn't. Usually I kept myself awake and occupied by making up or drawing my own comics. It was a habit I started way back in the ninth grade whenever I had a dull class and needed to pass the time quicker. I had drawn a lot of them over the years, and my friends and teachers both liked them. A couple of times I did that as part of an English project and received A's on both assignments. But this year, I had really cut down on my drawing since I was a senior and had more important things to do than drawing comics.

Like drawing pictures in my textbook or on my desk.

Like writing rap songs that didn't make sense.

Like worrying about girls who were considered crazy.

Like figuring out new ways to make the time go by faster.

"No, I haven't drawn anything. I've been thinking about (fill in the blank here) lately and wondering what's going to happen next."

I'd try to pay attention to Mr. Double C. the entire semester, but it was hopeless. I really did good to make C's in that class that year, especially when the class was at its hardest and dullest. I'd continue to ask Dave for help and anything else I could think of, just to make time go by faster.

Dave would either reply or go back to sleep and continue to make the highest grades in the class. I never could figure out how he did that. Maybe he was a mutant. But one thing I knew for certain: Calculus was the hardest and dullest class I would experience in my four years at Longview High, and I was glad to be rid of that class when the time came to graduate. (And no, it didn't help me no kind of way when I grew up.)

Tuesday, January 28

I was sitting in my 3rd period Radio-TV class when we were instructed via the intercom system to turn the TVs on to a network channel. We watched in silent horror the pictures of the space shuttle *Challenger* exploding in midair only minutes after takeoff. I could only sit there speechless and in shock as I thought of how the day before, watching on the news, I could see and almost feel the excitement of the crew and their families as they prepared for their mission. Now after this disaster, I said a silent prayer for those who had lost their loved ones and hoped they would find some sort of peace to be able to carry on in the future. For one day, everything was put in its proper perspective.

Friday, January 31

I was still having girl-problems. I tried to put my mind on Calculus, but that wasn't working. (I wonder why?) I had my SATs to worry about also, but that wasn't any big deal to me, either. I was trying to get over Annette, still had not really gotten over Kelly, and trying to avoid having to get over a third girl who just wouldn't leave me alone. To top it off, I also had the Round Table to worry about as I stupidly continued to sit with them at lunch, *and* I had yet another girl breathing down my neck trying to get me to go with her. I definitely wasn't lacking for attention.

Let's start with Annette. I really liked her, but there always seemed to be something, like a wall or a boyfriend, standing in between us. She'd call me every now and then, and we'd make plans to get together and do something friendly, like going to a movie or out to eat, but it would never happen.

"Hello?" I'd answer the phone then hear a familiar voice:

"Hi, friend, how're you doing?"

"Hey, Annette, what's up?"

"Oh, nothing. I was just calling to see what you were up to."

"I ain't doing nothing except watching TV. What're you up to?"

"I was just sitting here doing about the same. I was listening to somemusic earlier."

"What were you listening to?"

"Oh, some Janet Jackson..."

And on and on we'd talk, until one would invite the other over or something, and then we'd get off the phone and that would be that. I went to her house a couple of times, but she was never at home except one time, and we just stood in the yard and talked for a few minutes, then I left. Annette was basically a free spirit, and even though she sometimes gave the impression otherwise, I figured she preferred to remain that way, so I didn't try to change her mind about us.

About the other ex-girlfriend I hadn't gotten over yet, well, we'll get to her later.

Then there was Shelia. I was trying to figure her out, but I was really having trouble doing so. I had told her I wasn't really interested in us going together, especially since she had just broke up with one of my classmates, who was also a friend of mine. But she just wouldn't take no for an answer and continuously tried to get with me. I mean, she came over to my house three or four times looking for me afterschool, and two of those times I was fortunate enough to not be at home as I was hanging out with Dave both those times. But the other two times, she and her buddy Sonya caught me at home, but fortunately again, I only had to come outside once and speak to her. The other time, Momma, who could probably see what was happening or what was about to happen, told them I could not come out due to the extra homework I had (which was the truth, more than likely) and sent them on their way. However, the other time I was on my own.

"Hi, baby." Shelia always called me that, and I hated it for some reason.

"I'm not your baby," I said.

"One day, you will be. Won't he, Sonya?"

"Uh-huh."

"I don't think so," I said, "why won't you leave me alone? Can't you see that I'm not interested in you?"

"Stop lying, baby. If you weren't interested then why did you come over to my house two weeks ago? I haven't forgotten that, baby."

"For the last time, *I ain't your baby!* And I was just being...uh...just being friendly, that's all."

"Yeah, right. You looked more than friendly, if you ask me."

"Did he, girlfriend?" Sonya asked, smiling evilly.

"Sure did. I think he wanted something but he was trying to act all innocent about it, you know?"

I stood there as they laughed out loud, and then I asked: "What do you want?"

Shelia replied, "You *know* what I want."

That was what I was afraid of. "Let's walk over to the bridge, and we can discuss things there, *baby*," said Shelia as she grabbed my arm and started pulling me toward the creek.

I didn't know what to say. I was about to be "up the creek" both literally and figuratively. I was drowning and I needed help, fast. Then like the cavalry, someone came out of the house to my rescue.

"Cedric! Telephone for you!"

Flower-child might not have realized it (but then again, maybe she did), but she saved my you-know-what telling me I had a phone call. I went inside to take the call, while she stayed outside to talk to her friends. Sonya and Flower had known each other since they were in grade-school together. I don't remember who called, but by the time I got off the phone, Shelia and Sonya were gone back down the street, and Flower had come back in the house.

"Thanks a lot, sister."

"Uh-huh, yeah. Don't mention it. But I don't think Shelia is going to stop fooling with you anytime soon until you..."

"Yeah, yeah, yeah. Don't remind me." It was so hard to be a good person.

Monday, February 3

"What are you gonna do about that young girl who's been chasing you?"

Joyce looked at me across the table, actually expecting an answer. I thought, *"Now, how does she know about that? Oh wait, this is Joyce we're talking about here. She knows everything."* I ignored her, which actually was more dangerous than fooling with Shelia.

"I heard he talked to Annette on the phone Friday."

This time it was Wendy who spoke, knowing more about my business than she should have.

"How does Wendy know everything?" I thought, *"and worse, does she have to tell everybody, especially Joyce and Traci??"*

"You really are a Casanova, aren't you?" Joyce was starting to warm up. Before I could reply, Wendy said, "Not only that, but last semester in Economics class, Mr. Polawski called him *'Don Juan'* because he was over there trying to court Annette."

"Don Juan!? Ha Ha Ha Ha!"

"Did you say, Don Juan? HA HA HA!"

"'Don Juan' Edwards!! HA HA HA HA!"

"HA HA HA HA HA HA HA!!"

I looked at all of them as they enjoyed their little joke. "Ha-Ha, very funny. For that, I'm not going to answer any of your juvenile questions or say anything to y'all, period."

"Well, if y-you feel (ha-ha) that w-way," said Joyce, still shaking with laughter, "then get on from this table. BEGONE, Don JUAN!!!"

"HA HA HA HA! Later, crib-robber! HA HA HA!"

"Exit stage-right!! Ha Ha Ha!"

The Round Table nearly killed themselves with laughter.

Would've been nice if they had.

CHAPTER 14

The Senior Celebration

Sunday, February 9, 1986

I didn't go to the Senior Celebration the night before.

End of chapter.

OK, that would be kind of dull, and since this book is anything but dull, let's see why I didn't go.

First of all, a little background on what exactly is The Senior Celebration. Well, in a way, it's not really a celebration, not unless one wanted to celebrate we had but three months to go in school. Really, it was more or less a formal "coming-out" affair that the school held every year for the graduating seniors and their parents. A senior boy would escort a senior girl down a ramp in front of millions of people. (Just kidding; it just felt that way for some.) In reality, it was in front of hundreds or maybe a thousand people, including teachers, principals, parents, family members, PTA officials, board members, and, well, you get the picture. While this was going on, the Master of Ceremonies would list in detail that boy and girl's achievements and accomplishments over the past four years. Since we had like over 300 and something seniors that would obviously take awhile. But usually except for a few nervous classmates, it was fun and nice for everybody. There'd be entertainment (the choir would sing), acknowledgements, and of course, the class favorites would also be named that night. Then afterwards, the couples would either go out on a date or go to a party or do both. (And yes, some probably did "other things" also.) Everybody usually had a good time. Those that went, that is.

"So, Ced, why didn't you go?"

Devin had gone and had a good time, and he wanted to know why the other half of the House Rockers didn't show up. Well, it all started when...

Rewind back a few weeks ago back to December...

We all headed for the Little Theater. They had called all the seniors for a meeting. I already knew it was to be about the upcoming Senior Celebration in a month or so and I really wasn't very excited about it. The Senior Celebration was a tradition started back in 1978 to honor the seniors, and a part of the tradition was escorting a girl you had previously asked (sometimes years in advance) onto the floor. And since at this time there were only two girls who I wanted to ask to be my date and escort, and since one had already turned me down (she already had a date made from years past) and since I hadn't been bold enough to ask the other (she already had a date, too, anyway), I figured I wasn't going to be able to go anyway. And really, I didn't want to go.

Devin and I walked into the auditorium and sat down, and sure enough, the meeting was about the Senior Celebration. They gave all the guys little yellow cards and we were to write our names down and who our escort was going to be that night and turn them in sometime in January. I think Devin filled his out that same day as did most guys and turned it in, but I kept mine and took it home and tossed it somewhere. I didn't think about the Senior Celebration anymore until...

Fast forward to mid-January...

For once, I was concentrating on my studies and not thinking about girls period. Not until one Friday our student council president, Kenneth Lewis, came up to me in between classes.

"What's up, Cedric? You're just the man I need to talk to."

"Oh, really? What about?" I asked.

"I hear you're not going to the Senior Celebration. Or at least, thinking about not going. I noticed you didn't turn in your card."

"Yeah, that's right."

"Well, you know there are a lot of girls who want to go to the Senior Celebration but can't because they have no date. And we couldn't deprive them of that privilege, now could we?"

I already knew where this was going, for Ben and Ray, who also weren't going, had already warned me about Kenneth, his little speech, and his other little surprise. "No, I guess we couldn't." I decided to humor him. Devin was standing nearby looking with interest.

"OK. What I have here is a list of girls who want to go the event. You just look at this list and tell me which one you want to take out."

As I mentioned above, I knew he was going to try and talk me into going to the celebration and I knew he was going to pull out a list of girls who had no dates for obvious reasons (and not because they were too pretty-looking to have dates), so I wasn't too surprised. I looked at the list and didn't see anyone I was even remotely interested in. In fact, looking at the list made me not want to go even more! I told Kenneth, "Look, I don't think I can do this. I really don't want to go to the Senior Celebration."

"But why? This is something to look forward to. It's a tradition."

To me, tradition was winning football district titles, not going to the Senior Celebration. "Yeah, but I'm just not interested in going, that's all." That was an understatement.

"Well, I'll tell you what: you think about it over the weekend, and if you change your mind, let me know, and we'll get things rolling, OK?"

"OK." But I already knew I wasn't going, no matter what.

Wednesday, February 5

If anyone asked me how things were going, I would have said, "Well, they're just going." I had settled into a routine, my classes were set, it was time for the round stretch. This semester I was taking Government first period, English second period, Radio-TV third period, Calculus fourth period, Office-Aide fifth period, and Spanish sixth period. I had started making it a (bad) habit of sitting with the Round Table (Wendy, Robrina, Joyce, Traci, Chandra, and Diana) during lunch, Shelia was still trying to talk to me (and I was still trying to avoid her), I still played dominoes every now and then in the field house during lunch when I didn't feel like sitting with the Round Table usually with Devin or Kenneth Avery (he decided to switch sides and join a winner) as my partner, my classes were interesting (except for you-know-what-class), and I had finally, and for now, cut down on chasing girls. I just sat with the Round Table; I didn't try to go with them. That would've been suicide.

Which, speaking of the frivolous females, they really tried to make me sweat a couple of times. And they did a pretty good job of it, too. One time they wanted to know if I was going to the Senior Celebration, and when I told them no, they demanded to know why. I wanted to say, *Well, one of ya'll is sitting here right at this table who I really wouldn't mind taking out and being my escort, but she already has a date, so I'm just not going.* But of course, that would've been suicidal as well as stupid, so I told them I wasn't going because I was going to be out-of-town with my family.

Of course, they didn't believe it.

The next thirty minutes were spent with them basically lecturing me on the merits of going out with one of the girls who was on Kenneth L's list, and the (ahem) positive possibilities it could lead to. (Not going to go any further than that.) I started wondering if these girls were as wild as they sounded and in Joyce's case, looked. But I escaped with my dignity intact, and there were no other discussions about the Senior Celebration with them until after it had occurred.

The other time, though, I didn't escape and they got me pretty good. This day saw me sitting with them and trying to digest my lunch while listening to one of their interesting spiels. Across the room from us sat someone very familiar.

"Cedric, isn't that your mother?"

I turned around and looked, and sure enough, like a nightmare come true, there sat my momma, who happened to be subbing for one of the teachers, eating with some of the other teachers.

"Uh, yeah. Well, gotta go! See y'all later!" I tried to leave the table without even having touched my food.

"YOU GO over there and say HI to your MOMMA!" Joyce and Robrina both screamed. They knew my momma and were beginning to smell the blood like a couple of sharks.

"I - I really don't want to bother her. She's probably busy."

"You go over there, or we'll go over there for you. HEY MRS. EDWARDS!" Joyce was yelling loud enough to wake the dead, as usual.

"OK, OK! I'll go over there! Hold your horses. Dang!" As I got up and started walking, I thought to myself how I was never going to sit with those freaks again. The only reason I had done so was to be close to Traci, but now, not even that was worth this. I walked real slowly and looked back at the fiends, who were watching my every step. Finally, I got to where my momma was sitting, and she had her back to me. I tapped her on the shoulder.

"Hi Momma," I said it with all the enthusiasm of a winded turtle.

"Hello Cedric. How's it going there, boy?" Momma looked happy and in a good mood.

"Uh, great. Just great." Too bad my mood was the total opposite.

"That's good." Then to another teacher: "This is my son here. Say hello to Mrs. Richardson, Cedric."

I didn't want to tell anyone hi; I just wanted to get the heck out of the cafeteria fast. But I went on and said hello.

"Well, I gotta go back and eat. See you later," I said.

"Bye. Take care and have a good day the rest of the day." Momma looked like she wanted to kiss me goodbye, but I quickly walked off. I thought about walking out of the cafeteria totally but with the Round Table watching my every move and with Momma also watching me now, I didn't have much choice but to go back to my seat. When I reached it, the Round Table waved to my mom, who now looked shocked that I was sitting with six girls. But she waved back. Me, I wanted to crawl under the table. They really enjoyed that.

Now, during this time also, when Dave and I had intelligent discussions, they really were intelligent discussions. For instead of talking about girls, machine-gun theories, weird teachers, and the like, we were discussing what colleges and universities we wanted to attend when we graduated from high school. He was going to attend Southern Methodist University (S.M.U.). He had already taken a few courses at SMU before school started so he was way ahead. I was looking at trying to attend SMU myself, Lamar University, and a college I hadn't thought about until a week or so ago called Stephen F. Austin State University (SFA). Unfortunately, my SAT scores weren't high enough to get me accepted into SMU, and in the long run, that was probably a good thing anyway. However, I had a visit scheduled for Lamar in mid-March, and my chances on being accepted by Lamar were greater than those for SMU. I had wanted to go to SMU because Dave was going there and I'd always liked Dallas; it was one of the more progressive and entertaining cities around. (But as it turned out, it might have been a good thing I didn't go to SMU. Dave stayed at SMU for a little over two years before he left and moved to California and attended school there, and I don't think I was ready for Dallas anyway considering my driving skills at the time, which weren't all that great.)

Lamar University was located in Beaumont, which was a hop and a skip away from Port Arthur, the home of my favorite auntie. I liked the idea of being close to her and the fact that Beaumont was like a four-plus hour's drive from Longview, so I'd be somewhat far from home. But when I visited the campus later on, it wasn't as great as I thought it was. There seemed to be a lot of strange people walking around, and the atmosphere did not feel positive. "Are you sure you want to go here?" Flower-child asked. She had accompanied me on the trip, and even she sensed something was not right. "Uh, right now, I think I just want to get the heck out of here." I didn't mince no words, and we didn't waste any time doing that. We went to visit our aunt, then came back home. I don't think my parents liked Lamar all that much either, but only for the reason they didn't want me going to school that far, anyway.

At church, the previous Sunday, another friend of mine, Lawrence Carpenter came up to me and told me he was going to SFA.

"SF- what?" I replied, never really having heard of the school.

He repeated it and told me I should try to go there also, and that he would let me know more about the school at a later date.

That date was February 8, 1986, the same date as the Senior Celebration.

Saturday, February 8: The Night of the Senior Celebration

The day started interestingly enough; early this morning after everyone had left, Shelia came by knocking, determined to "do the do", so to speak, and I reacted by locking all the doors and closing all the blinds and letting her think no one was at home. Believe it or not, I really didn't want the girl, but I didn't want to hurt her feelings either, so I just played hard to get. I thought she'd never leave, but she finally left, and I spent the rest of the day thinking about the night's upcoming activities, which I was not going to be a part of. At 8 p.m., I had all but wrote off the entire evening when there was a knock at the door, and I began hoping it wasn't Shelia again. Fortunately it wasn't her. It was our class' resident ex-Lobo exile, Lawrence Eugene Carpenter.

"What's up, L.C.? What are you doing here?" I said, surprised at this unexpected visit.

"The real question ought to be, what are you doing here at home and not at the Senior Celebration, my friend."

"Well, I didn't have no date, and I just didn't feel like going anyhow, and you know how it is. I just felt like chillin' out tonight." Actually, I was starting to wonder to myself if I'd made a mistake by not going.

"Well, so-and-so's giving a party after all that is over with and I was going to go hang out over there for awhile. You want to come along?"

Strangely and also kind of contradictory, I just wasn't in the mood for being around a bunch of people at that moment. Not even some of my classmates.

"Nah, that's alright. Hey, tell me a little bit more about SFA before you go."

"That's right. Man, you ought to go there."

Lawrence had received a scholarship in football and was going to be attending SFA in the fall. I'd received brochures from SFA in the past but had never filled out any of the applications or forms that came with them. In other words, I'd never paid much attention to SFA. And I didn't know all that much about Nacogdoches, the town the college was in, except we'd always beat them in football and that it seemed to be a nice, quiet, old town. (Actually, it's a very historic town with a lot of nice scenery.) SFA seemed to be a pretty big school, from looking at some pictures. Lawrence had already visited there and liked it; the more he told me, the more I wanted to go find out for myself.

After he finished telling me about the school and asking again if I wanted to go to the party, (I declined) he left, and I immediately looked for the brochures and pamphlets I had gotten in the past from SFA. I found them after about an hour of searching, went on ahead and filled them out and I mailed my application in the next day.

Monday, February 10

"You should have seen it, Ced E.! I've never seen anything so funny in all my life!"

Devin, even now as he was saying this, was laughing hard enough to split a gut. "They came walking down the ramp after getting their names called out, there's bright lights everywhere, flashing, and he..." Devin paused trying to get ahold of himself. "He steps on her dress, which was too long anyway, he trips and falls and pulls her down, too! They must have knocked over half those lights. Ha Ha Ha Ha! I mean, we all died laughing! I thought I really was going to die. Ha Ha Ha! I'm dying now!" I just kind of smiled, a little sorry of the fact that I wasn't there to see that, and glad of the fact that it wasn't me who made a fool out of himself at Senior Celebration. Momma didn't raise no fool.

"Anyway, that really was the only thing that happened that was worth mentioning. I was just praying that I wouldn't walk out there and fall on my face in front of everybody like that because some of those girls' dresses were very, very long."

Devin continued, "I'll tell you what, though. The girl who looked the best was someone you'd never expect...Velecia Stanton." Somehow, I was surprised and not so surprised at the same time. Velecia had always had a "hidden beauty" to me, and I'd wondered in the past what she would look like if she let it show more. Obviously, she must have looked real good.

"Then you missed the party. You won't believe this, but then again, maybe you will, but Lois stood up Ron after the Celebration." Again, I wasn't too surprised.

"That kind of sucked."

"Yeah, it did."

"Why didn't you go to the Senior Celebration?"

"Devin," I said looking real serious, "you've just answered your own question."

Later.

CHAPTER 15

A Star is Born

Thursday, February 13, 1986

"Are you sure you want to do this?" Flower-child asked.

"Yeah, I'm sure. Give me one," I said. I looked at the red decorated paper after it was handed to me. "That'll be one dollar," said the student, and I gave it to him.

Flower-child shook her head. "I think you should leave well enough alone."

"I think you should be quiet, small fry."

Flower-child stood by me, watching with a small amount of interest, as I began arranging and rearranging the materials I had purchased. "Who's it going to be for?" she asked, "and don't tell me it's for…"

"It's NOT," I interrupted, knowing full well who she was talking about. "It's for someone else. Someone special." I took out a pen and started writing in my neatest handwriting on the "vale-gram." 'Roses are red, violets are blue, I hope this Valentine's Day is special for you.' Then I wrote on the front of a small card: 'To Traci, From Cedric'. I took out a small box of candy I had gotten the day before and placed all three together neatly and wrapped it with a ribbon and handed back to the student, who then left on his mission.

"Traci? Who is Traci? Is she one of those girls I saw you sitting with in the cafeteria last week?" Flower-child now was more than a little curious.

"Maybe."

"Which one is she? Wait a minute. She's got to be the pretty one with the long hair and the nice smile. In fact, she spoke to me and asked me if I was your sister. It's her, isn't it?"

"Maybe."

"I bet…no…I KNOW she has a boyfriend…somewhere. Are you crazy doing this? Why are you doing this?"

"Oh, I don't know…" And really, *I didn't know*.

"Sometimes," I said looking and trying to sound kind of mysterious, "you just want to see which way the wind is blowing. Know what I mean, Flowers?"

Flower-child wasn't buying it. "No, I don't know what you mean. Sometimes I think you ain't got it all. Know what *I* mean, big brother?"

I ignored her and went on to Radio-TV class.

"So tell me: how does it feel being a major superstar in the recording industry?" Craig Wynn wanted to know.

"You know, I try not to let these things go to my head, but I'd be lying if I said it's no big deal. I feel I am the best this industry has to offer." The class snickered as I said this in a voice maybe five or six octaves higher than my normal voice.

"Uh huh. Do you think your success can be attributed to the time you spent at *Motown*?"

"*Motown* had NOTHING to do with my success. What I accomplished, I accomplished on my own. I am a very talented individual, you know."

"Despite your handicap."

"It wouldn't have mattered if I had two or three fingers on each hand missing *and* was blind!! I can play a dozen instruments a dozen different ways. You haven't heard anything until you've seen me play an organ with my mouth! I used to turn out the church!" the class laughed.

"I imagine you did "turn out" church," Craig said, and the class laughed harder.

"What? Man, are you trying to be funny?" I said with mock anger.

"No, no. Well, it was a pleasure having you here today. Are you going to do a song for us?"

"But of course. I brought my harmonica."

"Well, all-right. Ladies and gentleman, here he is, the man himself: Little Stacy Wonderful!"

Then I broke into the worst-ever version of the song, *I Just Called to Say I Love You*, anyone ever heard. I butchered it some more trying to play the harmonica to it. Needless to say, I could not play the harmonica. Nor could I sing. And the class died laughing. This was part of my radio-TV class. We were learning how to do talk shows and interviews that week. Craig was playing a talk-show/interviewer host, and I was playing a famous recording star. It was someone we made up, as one could tell, right? The class loved it. They loved it so much that they wanted "Little Stacy Wonderful" to make a return appearance in some of the rest of the class' various skits. I had never considered myself a funny person, but a lot of my classmates had never seen me act this silly before and they naturally thought it was real funny.In fact, our teacher, Mrs. Paul, really encouraged us to be as creative as we wanted, as long as we didn't do anything vulgar or ridiculous. I got to show a different side of me in that class, one that only Flower-child and a few of my closest friends knew about before, and that class was really fun! Think about it: I could make an A in the class just by acting stupid!

We did radio programs where we each got to create our own radio-stations, call-letters, commercials, and were our own disc jockeys. We did our own television news programs, created TV commercials, and of course, created our own television shows. We learned how to use television cameras and all the techniques that go into radio-TV production. Like I said, it was a very fun class.

Besides the "Little Stacy" bit, I also made a "swatch" commercial. (Whatever happened to swatches anyway?) Me and two girls, Sandra Bolden and Lissa Warren, were singing and rapping and unfortunately, dancing about swatches. No, I wasn't the second coming of James Brown. Nothing more needed to be said about that. Then some of my classmates and I decided to do a version of *The Newlywed Game*. I happened to be "married" to this girl named Falecia Woods. Needless to say, I think we might have gotten one question right: *Did y'all make whoopie on your honeymoon night?* The answer definitely wasn't "no," and fortunately, my "wife" and I agreed on that. (Thanks Falecia, whereever you are.) Anyway, that was interesting to say the least.

Friday, February 14

Of course, it was Valentine's Day, and I waited to see what the fruits of my labor would be. They didn't deliver the vale-grams and gifts until fourth period, so over half a day went by before I found out anything. No, I didn't sit with the Round Table on Valentine's Day. I did not want to die on Valentine's Day. After a while I saw Traci walking towards class with some roses and a card, and I thought to myself, *Where did those come from?* Then I thought, *Oh well, maybe she did get something from her boyfriend.* Finally, Robrina came up to me before fifth period and told me that Traci got the candy and vale-gram I sent and that she liked it and thought it was nice, but she also told me something else:

"Did you know that Devin sent her some roses and a card?"

Hmmmm. Well, like they say, '*All's fair in love and war.*' Really, though, I wanted to strangle Devin.

However, in the long run, Devin actually did me a favor. For a little while, during lunch, I had either been sitting with the Round Table or going down in the field house to go play dominoes. Devin had a different lunch period now, so I mainly would team with Kenneth to play some unlucky individuals. But though Kenneth and I won our share our games, we also lost our share. The main culprits usually were Harold and Tony Simmons. They really tried to punish us, and I had to admit I learned quite a few lessons from them. Half of the time, Kenneth and I were plainly out of synch, and most of the time, I was the one who was struggling. But as the saying went, *'you have to crawl before you can walk'*, and this was a good example of that, for taking my share of the beatings made me a better player in the long run. With me spending more time doing this and courting girls who I had no chance with, my schoolwork began to suffer.

So, after Valentine's Day, it was time for more changes. I would stop playing dominoes at school for the rest of the year while trying to get my classes and grades in order. In fact, I had a lot of tests, projects, and research papers coming up and I needed to concentrate on those. Therefore, no more dominoes.

And, somewhat shockingly, no more worrying about girls. I finally got some common sense and stopped sitting with the Round Table. Since Traci seemed to be interested in Devin and vice versa, I didn't feel I needed to worry about Traci anymore. Besides, she was in good hands. (Thanks Devin.) And even though Shelia bothered me every now and then, she really wasn't a problem. Annette had faded away, so I was finally "to myself." Flower-child had a boyfriend now, so she wasn't around too much to bother me. I figured the rest of the year was going to be a piece of cake until graduation. No more distractions, no more "machine-gunning," no more worrying. I would concentrate on school and nothing else. Yeah, right.

Thursday, February 27

Flower-child came into my room. "What's up, big brother?" she asked. I sat on the bed staring blankly at part of my homework. It was probably

Calculus. I sighed then I spoke: "Deshane Woodson spoke to me this morning."

Flower muttered, "Aww, no."

Deshane was Kelly's sister.

"She said I should try to call Kelly. She said that Kelly is going to be my date for the prom."

Flower looked at me and shook her head and walked out the room. I thought, *Here we go again..*

CHAPTER 16

No Hablo Espanol, I Only Take It

March-April, 1986

My sixth period class, Spanish II, was the wackiest class I had ever taken in my life. Radio-TV was great, but this class was something else.

Let's begin with the teacher. Mrs. McCalley, God rest her soul, was one of the funniest and most laid-back teachers I had ever seen. And with a class like the one she had this period, she had to be. She could have wrote up everybody and been justified in doing so, but she realized that the students in the class were basically a fun-loving bunch, although mischievous most of the time, and that we did actually try to learn something and do our work when we were supposed to. The bottom line is, Mrs. McCalley was really a cool teacher who made the class fun instead of something not to look forward to.

Another trait we appreciated about Mrs. McCalley was that not only did she not take us too seriously, but she didn't take herself too seriously either, obviously. It was not uncommon for her to go take one of her "teacher lounge breaks" right before class started and leave us seniors who were in the class in charge. (Talk about instant authority!) The class was made up of mostly sophomores, a few juniors, and three of us seniors. (Don't ask me why we were taking the class; I guess we just needed the credit.) And whenever Mrs. McCalley had something to do or check on, she usually left me and the other two seniors in charge. One of the seniors was one of the coolest guys in school, if not the coolest. The other senior was a girl who acted more like a sophomore than anything, so I guess she always got overlooked. For a little while, anyway. More on her a little later. Before we get into what being put in charge of an entire class was like, let me tell you about the other senior guy in the class, Mr. "Super Cool," Curt Vines.

If Curtis Vines hadn't been in my Spanish class that year, I think that the class would've suffered for it. In fact, if he hadn't been in two of my other classes (Office-Aide and Calculus), I probably would've never gotten to know him and been worse off for it. He turned our senior-year into a one-man trip-out show. I had never seen anyone who could be so cool and yet so funny at the same time. Before I met him, I had viewed him as one of those guys who were stuck on themselves because the girls were so crazy about them. Even my sister thought he was real handsome. Curt, in fact, had been voted most handsome in our class almost every year. But he was not a stuck-up individual; anything but, and really one of the nicest and down-to-earth guys you'd ever meet. After I got to know him, I realized that even though he looked serious most of the time and could somewhat be considered a cynic, it was his cynicism and his ability not to take life (and school) seriously and joke about it that made him someone I liked hanging around with. Really and truly, he had me laughing _every day._ His viewpoint of our final year at LHS was basically, 'Let's get the heck outta Dodge while the getting's good.' Whereas in the past, he had concentrated and studied hard and made excellent grades, this year he plainly didn't give a you-know-what. He wasn't taking anything seriously this year. And he'd tell you to your face, too, that he didn't care. It was just the way that he did it that was so funny and so cool. He usually had to punctuate his rantings with a cussword or two, and it was just plain hilarious to hear him talk that way. For example: "Cedric, you know I don't give a <bleep> about this class." he'd tell me, sneering all the while. "I'm just taking it just to be taking something. What, are we all going to be speaking <bleeping> Spanish someday? (Possibly) Like, it's going be our national language in the future? (Maybe) Yeah, right. Give me a <bleeping> break. They don't want me speaking Spanish. I'd be cussing somebody out." And on and on he'd go, ragging on our Spanish class, but not really being serious about it, and I'd try to keep from laughing too hard or too loud.

So whenever Mrs. McCalley left us in charge, Curt would go and stand up front and tell everybody, "I don't care what y'all do. If you want to leave, then get the heck out of here!" Or, if he was really in a "foul" mood, he'd tell the class to open their books and do all the questions in "<bleeping> chapters ten thru sixteen...NOW." Of course, no one really took him seriously; the few that *did*, however, would look at me sitting at the teacher's desk with my feet upon the desk as if the desk had my name on it or something and would wonder if Curt was serious or not. "Better do what he says, y'all," I would deadpan, "or it might get ugly up in here." The class would then look at us and then laugh, until we took out the paddle and went to work. (Just kidding.) Of course, I wasn't serious; just looked it. And Curt probably looked more serious than I did, but inside was probably about to burst out laughing.

Another time, Curt and I gave hallway passes to everyone and told the class to get the heck out. The class did what we told them to do, of course, and left. We were going to leave too. But luckily, Mrs. McCalley got back just in time. Don't worry; we weren't being disrespectful or anything like that. The class didn't get too far, around the corner actually, and they all came back in a matter of seconds. It just a good joke on a good teacher. And she didn't get angry, just even. She made all of us write 1000 times not to do something like that again...in Spanish, of course. (Again, I'm just kidding. It was a hundred times.) Like I said, you couldn't take anything we did too seriously. But while Curt and I were using the class to improve our people skills, the other senior in the class was using the class to improve her people skills with yours truly.

I'd known Randressa Roberts off and on in the past, had a few classes with her here and there, and really hadn't paid that much attention to her. So it came as a surprise when I found out that she obviously liked me a lot. You'd think with all these different girls liking me off and on I'd keep a girlfriend, but not necessarily so. Kelly and Randressa had been real good friends with one another for a long, long time, but I guess when she saw that Kelly was out of the picture (for now, anyway), she figured she could move into the picture and really tried her best to get my attention. "Call me Randi," she told me one day when we happened to be working together on a paper. I looked at her and I thought I was seeing things, but the girl had love in her eyes. "Okay, Randi it is. Uh-huh. Right. Ran-di." I said. She wasn't bad-looking, she had medium-length hair, was bright-skinned, and had a decent shape and face, but she just wasn't my type, not that it made any difference to her.

One time while I was busy sitting at the teacher's desk enjoying all the power that came with it, she came and hopped into my lap and put her arms around me and tried to convince me she was the one for me, instead of Kelly. I'm thinking, *This is one of Kelly's friends?* Again, all's fair in love and war, but this was ridiculous. As she sat in my lap hugging my neck (and this was during class, mind you; the rest of the class didn't know whether to laugh or cry or what), I squirmed uncomfortably. The last thing I wanted to do was get excited over this. Curt came over and said to Randi, "And what *is* Santa getting you for Christmas this year? Looks like to me he's already got his gift!" the whole class exploded with laughter. I don't know, but maybe I did look like Santa considering how red I got.

And speaking of "unusual" moments involving Curt and Randi, another time we were busy doing a worksheet in class, and Curt leaned over and whispered, "Hey Cedric!"

"Yeah, what?" I was so totally immersed in my work that I didn't look up or turn.

"You need to go get that."

"Get what?" I said, still not looking.

"Look in front of you."

Our desks happened to be arranged in four rows that day, with each row facing each other forming a sort of box. Which meant I was facing another desk...and in it sat Randi. I glanced at her and went back to doing what I was doing.

"Yeah, right. It's Randi," I thought Curt was trying to be funny, as usual.

"Look again," he said, "take a reeeeal long look at her."

I sighed and looked up again and saw Randi, who was looking right at me with kind of a silly grin on her face. *OK, she's grinning at me. That's not unusual...*But then I noticed what Curt was talking about...in spades. I did a double-take. "Holy <Bleep>!" I almost yelled, becoming Curt for a millisecond.

Randi just happened to be wearing a white mini-skirt which just happened to be, to put it bluntly, shorter than average, and since she was sitting facing me, she decided to give me a pretty good view of things by sitting with her legs spread wide open. Like I said, she wasn't the prettiest or ugliest girl one I'd ever seen, but from the neck and waist down, things were looking pretty good.

Instantly, I forgot everything---what day it was, what time it was, what class I was in, what kind of work I was doing, what my name was--everything! I was totally mesmerized, until Mrs. McCalley walked over to me and asked me if I was alright. I thought to myself, *No, I'm not alright! I'm sitting here losing my innocence...*No, seriously, I mumbled something like, "What? Huh?" I was totally out of it. Meantime, Curt was snickering like crazy and Mrs. McCalley figured Curt must have told me something crazy, so she asked him what was going on, and he replied, "Nothing. Ced is probably high or something. He'll be alright." So she walked away wondering what did Curt say or do <u>this time</u>. Randi, by this time, was sitting with her legs closed, but after Mrs. McCalley walked away, she opened them again and motioned to me. Curt, who couldn't pass this opportunity up, whispered to me, "Go get her, Cedric! She wants you." "She's calling you---'*Cedric, come get me and make me happy!*'" he said that in such a silly voice, I couldn't help but laugh. But truth be told, I almost really did want to jump out of my desk.

Curt, Randi, and I also did a Spanish project one time where we did a TV show entirely in Spanish. I (somehow) was able to put together giant backgrounds of the school I drew and colored myself while trying to keep from laughing too hard at Curt and his insane jokes on one hand and keeping Randi restrained from sexually assaulting me with the other hand. The backgrounds turned out to be 6'x6' drawings of the campus of LHS; it took me a couple of weeks to draw and color the pictures. Curt and Randi wrote the story, one half drama and violent, the other half romantic, and I played the victim (obviously). It was fun, for them mainly. Curt must have killed my character half a dozen times, and Randi hugged me so much I thought I was at church. She really wanted to be bolder than that, But Mrs. McCalley said, *"No way, Jose."* So it was what it was: Nearly R-rated. I was more proud of the backgrounds I did than my acting-I only wish I had kept them. (I gave them to Randi as a kind of gift.) Sometimes, she really did make me want to think about her…

<u>Anyway</u>**,** even though Curt would get me from time to time, he was very relentless when it came to Nina Blue's little sister, Pookie. Yep, I hate to say it, but she was asking for it with a name like that. Pookie was a sophomore, and like her sister, she was very nice and not too bad-looking. Unlike her sister, who was a Viewette, Pookie was a majorette. Curt and Nina had been friends for awhile, and I guess Pookie felt that Curt and she would be the same kind of friends. Instead, Curt would razz Pookie almost every chance he got. One time Pookie told us about the time she went to some kind of class or camp for majorettes that was being held at a nearby college. She and a large group of girls had to go to the school auditorium and hear one of the instructors give a speech about dancing and twirling a

baton at the same time or something like that. While she was sitting there listening, she said she felt someone rub on her legs from behind, and when she turned to look, of course there were nothing but girls sitting behind her and all of them just looked at her. She turned back around to face the instructor, and *again,* someone felt on her. She turned again and everyone just looked at her *again.* (This would have made a great *Twilight Zone* episode.) She said it freaked her out so bad, she left the building and went back to her room before the speech was over. I had some sympathy for her, but Curt had none:

"Aww, you know you liked that," he said.

"What!?" Pookie was mortified, "no, I didn't!"

"Who you trying to fool? You need to come out of the closet," Curt turned and looked at me and said real seriously, "Pookie's a lesbian."

Pookie nearly exploded, "NO, I'm NOT! I can't believe this."

"Believe it," Curt muttered, "Pookie's a nasty lesbian." I was trying hard not to laugh, but I couldn't help it. Curt looked so serious saying this you would've thought he was quoting a scripture from the Bible. What was so funny was that Pookie was actually taking him seriously and reacting thusly.

"How…how can you say that? I like BOYS, not girls," said Pookie. He had turned red and looked as if she was going to cry.

"Easily. Hey, Scott! Did you know that Pookie's a lesbian?"

Scott answered, "No, I didn't. How did you find out?"

"Heck, she just sat here and told us."

"Well, I swear."

Pookie looked as though she swallowed a dead armadillo. She shook her head and said, "Why are you saying this for? You know I'm not."

Curt replied, "I don't know that. And I'm saying this because I guess I just like you." Then he looked around at Scott and me, winked, then turned to Pookie and said, "NOT!"

Curt never did forget that story Pookie told us and he continuously kept Pookie from forgetting it, too. Towards the end of school year one nice, breezy day, he told Scott, "You know, we can't get Pookie drunk because she's liable to go chasing after women or something." Scott laughed as Pookie turned around.

"What did you say?" she asked.

Curt continued talking to Scott acting as if he hadn't heard her speak: "I think if Pookie had maybe, hmmm, a beer and a half, it might start her to feeling on people's legs in here."

Scott said, "You think?"

"Yeah. Then she might get overly excited. Know what I mean?"

Scott shook his head yes as he tried to keep from laughing out loud.

Pookie turned red...again. And was speechless.

Curt looked at her and said, "And *we* wouldn't want that to happen, now would *we*?"

Once again, a group of us had to do a play totally in Spanish about anything we wanted. As long as it wasn't about anything obscene or stupid. This narrowed things down quite a bit for ol' Curt. My group, which consisted of myself, Curt, Scott, and Randi--the three seniors plus one junior--decided to do a news program. We called it "Channel Siente News," or something like that. We was going to do news stories on ridiculous things, such as *"Boy and his Dog Blow Up Empty School"* or *"Man Hit By Invisible Bus."* As you might've guessed, Curt was in charge of writing the script. I designed and drew the backgrounds again. (I think I gave these to Randi also afterwards. She liked my drawers, I mean, drawings.) Randi and Scott would play the parts of the news anchors. Even though we tried our best to get really silly with it, Mrs. McCalley kept us under control. We still had a lot of fun with the project even though Mrs. McCalley had a hard time keeping Curt under control. Curt kept trying to ask Mrs. McCalley what the Spanish words were for words like...well, let me give y'all a few examples:

Curt: *Mrs. McCalley! What is "butt-hole" in Spanish?*

Mrs. McCalley: **What?? What are you writing about?**

Curt: *I want to say, "The light had turned red, but the butt-hole ran the light anyway and hit the Budweiser truck."*

Mrs. McCalley: **Forget it, Curt.**

Or:

Curt: *Mrs. McCalley!*

Mrs. McCalley: ***Yes, Curt?***

Curt: *How do I say this in Spanish: "The fire gutted the condom factory and all the rubbers went up in smoke."*

Mrs. McCalley: **<u>No</u>, Curt.**

Somehow we got the thing written, and the "play" (if you want to call it that) turned out to be pretty good. I think Curt may have snuck in a questionable word or two, but with it being in Spanish, I don't think anyone noticed, save our teacher, and even she might not have been totally paying attention. It was an easy 100 for a test grade at that. Worked for me.

Towards the end of the year, Curt *really* got unmotivated. We'd be doing worksheets in class or for homework, and Curt would be sitting there scribbling on his worksheet. I was taking my work seriously, so I'd help him with his so he wouldn't get too many bad grades. As it were, though, it was hard for him to stay motivated, and he tried to find ways to amuse himself (and others). One time, we were all working on a worksheet in class, or I should say, all of us but one. Curt sat there playing with his pen, and then said to me, "This is some boring crap." We were reading a story in Spanish and having to answer questions about it. "I know what I'm fixing to do: I'm going to liven this baby up a bit."

In the next few minutes, he changed the story into something totally x-rated complete with pictures drawn by him (and he *cannot* draw) and wrote down the most ridiculous answers I'd ever seen. Mrs. McCalley had decided that we were going to grade each other's papers for a daily grade, and when I looked at Curt's paper, I nearly fell out of my seat. "What is THIS?" I whispered kind of loudly.

Curt replied, "Call it, *'Detective Hombre Meets Senorita Ellena'*."

I laughed so hard I nearly fainted. That did not help his grade any, and he didn't get any of the questions right, and of course, he didn't really care. Mrs. McCalley wanted to take up the worksheets, but I just did not have the heart (nor the guts) to give her Curt's, so I just said he didn't do his. (Which, when you think about it, he hadn't.) So she gave him another sheet, and he halfway did it the second time around.

There were some other characters in that class; such as the two Davids: David Morriston and David Bertram. They were both tenth-graders at this time and had been friends since they were pre-schoolers. They kind of reminded me of Butch Cassidy and the Sundance Kid; Very seldom did I not see them together. Besides Randi, there were these two other girls who were like members of my fan club: Devitra Figures and Tiana Mack. Like the two Davids, both girls were sophomores, and while Devitra was more like a friend to me (and a crazy one at that), I think that Tiana kind of liked me from a distance and wanted to be a little more than just a friend, but not to the extremes like Randi did. Tiana was more reserved and quiet, but she and I talked a few times during class (and even worked together) and I thought she was a very down-to-earth intelligent person. If I had a choice of picking her or Randi, I would have picked Tiana. Devitra was sillier and crazier than Tiana, and she liked picking on both Davids whenever she could, which really wasn't a good idea, since they'd been friends since forever and knew how to double-team someone. But Devitra could take it as well as dish it out, and they all got along. The four of them would usually try to give me a hard time whenever I played teacher, and I'd threaten to move their desks away from each other if they kept up the smart-talk. Nine times out of ten, Curt and I would end up moving their desks. I'd try to put Devitra by me, and she'd would either pinch or kick me to stop me from moving her desk. No, I didn't try to move Tiana's desk by me (I should have), and definitely not Randi's desk, for obvious reasons. I knew Devitra would put up a fight, so that made it more fun and more interesting in more ways than one.

Really, this was the perfect class to end the day with, for more often than not, I would leave that class with a smile on my face or stumble out of it laughing. And considering how some of my days went, I really needed to laugh.

CHAPTER 17

Kelly and Me, Part 3

Monday, March 3, 1986

As I mentioned before, I had finally decided to stop playing dominoes at school and sitting with the Round Table during lunch, and I began to concentrate solely on grades when I had an unexpected visitor to my first period class. I hadn't even been thinking about the upcoming prom next month, until now:

"I've got a message for you," Deshane Woodson said, "you're taking my sister to the prom." Her sister happened to be Kelly, the girl who had dumped me twice over the last four months. And I wasn't necessarily looking or planning for it to happen a third time. I hadn't really thought about Kelly too much since Homecoming obviously, nor was I in any hurry to do so. I looked at Deshane and said, "Huh? What did you say?"

"I said, "You're going to be taking Kelly to the Prom. You're going to be her date. Well, gotta go to class. See you later." As Deshane walked away, I thought to myself, *She has got to be kidding*. And unless Kelly had changed over the last few months, she didn't really like me anyway, and the feeling was currently mutual.

Well, obviously, something had changed, for Kelly came up and spoke to me after lunch and we wound up walking to class together. She wanted to know had I asked anyone out to the prom yet, and I hadn't and told her so. She then wanted to know if we could actually go to the prom *together*. She sure didn't waste any time. I really wasn't all that sure, so I told her I'd think about it. (*Surprise!*)

The bottom line was that I didn't really trust her and she had already burned me in the past, twice at that. So I really didn't want to start back talking to her. BUT...then again, deep down, I did still have some feelings for her and maybe, just maybe, things would work out between us. Let's face it: I was confused. And I really wasn't too enthused about the whole deal either. Kelly could see this, for when I tried to talk to her before 6th period, she gave me the cold shoulder.

So, today I figured this was not going to work and if she was going to be acting funny, seemingly not wanting to speak and all that, at least this time I was going to beat her to the punch. This time, I left a note in *her* locker stating that it was over (before it had ever gotten started, of course). I didn't want to talk to her anymore, and that I definitely wasn't taking her to the prom. Let her find another idiot--I was through playing the part.

Wednesday, March 5

"You stupid idiot," my sister glared at me, "why should you feel bad about what you did? Better to learn a lesson the easy way now than to learn it the hard way later on. I can't believe you."

Flower-child looked at me as though she wanted to strangle me. I felt as though I needed strangling. Because, for some unknown reason, I was starting to feel guilty about the note I had placed in Kelly's locker. Kelly hadn't said anything to me yesterday or today, but I figured she got the note, and I don't know, maybe I had hurt her feelings or something. "Hurt HER feelings? You've got to be kidding! What about YOUR feelings? Kelly doesn't really talk to you, she acts as if you don't exist, makes a fool out of you, all in ONE week, and YOU"RE feeling guilty??" Flower-child looked at me. "You must be brain damaged."

"No, I'm not. Look, I can't explain it," I said, "but I just don't think I should have done her like that. Maybe she has changed. Maybe not. But I think I should give her a chance, at least."

"Your funeral", my sister said, and I hoped she was wrong about that.

Friday, March 7

I stuck a note of apology in Kelly's locker this morning, and this evening I went by her house to talk to her. She told me she accepted my apology (even though she still hadn't apologized for her actions in the past) and that she still wanted us to go to the prom together. In fact, it seemed that her parents wanted us to go together even more so than she did. They were happy to see me when I visited, so happy it was almost strange. I had heard that even though Kelly wanted to go to the prom, her parents were not going to allow her to go unless she went with yours truly. (Of course, her parents liked me. What was there *not* to like?) So now, I was really starting to question whether or not Kelly wanted to go with me to the prom and not someone else and that maybe she was being forced into going with me. The whole thing did not make me feel too good.

Thursday, March 13

This week's top two questions have been: 1. Is Kelly using me (again)? And, 2. Who *am* I going to the prom with?

The latter question was the subject of debate on the bus this past Tuesday. Velecia Stanton, the star of the Senior Celebration and the girl with the voice deeper than mine, was sitting next to me, and she asked me the million-dollar question. "To be honest, I'm not sure yet," I said. Then Velecia said something that sincerely shocked me...

"I heard you were going with Traci Richards."

"Say *what*?"

"Don't you and Traci go together?" Velecia was serious.

"No, we've never gone together. Who told you that?" I was kind of curious to say the very least to find out where she got this information from.

"It's just something I heard. I thought that since y'all were going together, that y'all were going to the prom together."

"No, we don't go together, and I'm not taking her to the prom. I really don't know if I'm going to the prom or not." I said.

Suddenly, a voice cut in behind us: "He'd better not be taking anyone else to the prom...because he's supposed to be taking me!" I didn't have to look back to see who it was; I already knew...Shelia.

"Who is she?" Velecia asked, looking back at Shelia sort of strangely.

"Just ignore her," I said. "I'm not taking her either. Like I said, I'm not sure if I'm going or not." Shelia continued to rant and rave for a little while afterwards, but I didn't even acknowledge anything she was saying. My sister, however, heard her, and when we got home, she wanted to know what was going on. After I told her, Flower didn't look toosurprised.

"So, Shelia actually likes you. I thought she was playing around myself, but it sounds as if she's serious. Did you tell her you were going to take her to the prom?"

"What do you think? No."

"Well, if you do wind up going to the prom, who are you going to the prom with? And please don't say Kelly."

"Right now, I don't know." And I left it at that.

Friday, March 14

Today, Micheal, who had heard different rumors himself, asked me the million-dollar question and the two-million dollar question. "Are you going to the prom?" he asked while we were sorting out papers during office aide class.

"I'm not sure if I am or not. I've still got things to figure out."

"You're trying to figure out if Kelly is using you or not, right? Well, don't waste too much time doing so because while you're doing that, there are plenty of other girls who'd love to go out with you to the prom. I've heard some names being tossed around."

"Yeah, so have I."

"What are you feeling? Do you think she's going to screw you again?"

"I don't know. I'm not sure. Sometimes I think I'm making a big mistake trusting her again, and sometimes I feel I ought to give her another chance." I was really confused, to say the least.

"You really like her, don't you? This is different from Annette, ain't it?"

I shook my head yeah and thought, *It was different, but I'd be darned if I can figure out why.*

And speaking of Annette, as I was packing my clothes for tomorrow's trip to Beaumont, the phone rang. "Cedric, it's for you." I took the phone from my sister, who just shook her head.

"Hello?"

"Hi, Cedric. How are you doing?" It was Annette!

"Fine, how are you?" I hadn't talked to her since February. Why was she calling now? (As if I couldn't guess.)

"I'm doing fine. You haven't called or talked to me at school and I was just seeing how you were doing and if I'd done anything to make you mad or something."

"Of course not," I said, *But you could have went to the Senior Celebration with me instead of Robert.* I didn't say that out loud, but I thought it.

"Good. I've been hearing a lot of things about you and the prom. Are you going?"

"I really don't know." I was getting tired of the question.

"Well, I didn't think you were going and I didn't really believe all those stories about you going with some other girls, but I figured I had to hear it from you."

No, you didn't think I was going because I didn't ask you if you wanted to go. I was thinking some mean thoughts. "Well, I don't know anything right now, but as soon as I find out, I'll let you know, Ok? I'm sorry I can't stay on the phone too long right now, but I'm getting ready to go out-of-town tomorrow and I've still got some packing to do."

"Alright, but don't forget about me, ok? Call me when you get back."

"OK. Take care."

"Bye."

Wednesday, March 19

Today I decided to test the waters; I asked Kelly to go with me. As in, be my girlfriend. She said, *"I don't know."* The prom is a month from now, Friday, April 18th. And I was no closer to figuring out what to do. Kelly wasn't making it any easier, either. Like Micheal said, there were other girls who wanted to go with me to the prom (and probably go with me period), and here I was probably wasting my time with Kelly. Was I?

Spring Break: March 23 thru March 30

I didn't do much of anything during Spring Break, except sit around the house and decide what to do. I made the decision that I _did_ want to go to the prom since I missed out on the Senior Celebration, but the question of whom I was going to take out had yet to be answered. *Do I go with Kelly to the prom? Or, do I go with someone else?* Shelia still was under the influence I wasn't going to take anyone out but her, Randi had been trying to tempt me into taking her out, Annette seemed to want to rekindle something sometimes, and then there were others (like some of my sister's freshmen classmates) who felt they had an opportunity also.

I went over to Devin's house to play dominoes Thursday, and his take on the situation was: "Why not put all the names in a hat and pick out one?"

"Oh, come on. What if I pick out the name of someone I really *don't* want to take?" I could see myself picking Shelia's or Randi's name out of a hat first time out.

"Don't put their names in there in the first place, then. Come on, Ced, really, how hard is it to decide who to take out to the prom?" Devin looked smug, a little too smug.

"Really?" I glared at him. "Tell me: Who are <u>you</u> going with to the prom?"

"Well, I...uh...I haven't really decided if I'm going or not."

"And you talk about me being wishy-washy! Look at you!"

"You've got girls wanting to go with you; I don't have anybody asking me to take them to the prom like you do."

"What about Valecia? She's your girlfriend, isn't she?"

"Well, she might be a little too young for this sort of thing..."

"What do you mean, *a little too young*? She's only a year younger than me!"

"Obviously you're both baby chickens. But enough about my problems, we're discussing your problems. What about Annette? You two did go together, you know. I think she still likes you."

I slammed a domino down. "You always say that."

"And what about what's-her-name? Carrie? Kelsey?"

"It's Kelly, you wimp."

"Yeah, Kelly. Why won't you take her to the prom? Oh, I forgot. She made you look like an idiot at Homecoming. Wasn't hard to do, however."

I stared at him, and he laughed, "Just playing, little man. I don't know who you should take out or what you should do. Flip a coin or something."

"Thanks, Devin, you've been a lot of help. By the way," I gently laid down a domino, "that's twenty and that's game."

Devin's smile disappeared.

Wednesday, April 2

Today, *my* smile disappeared.

I had had enough. I told Kelly that I didn't want to see her anymore, I was through with her, and of course, I wasn't taking her to no prom. Like Flower-child said, it didn't make sense to constantly try to talk to and be nice to someone when they either ignored you or treated you like you were a disease. I didn't know what Kelly's problem was, and right about now, I didn't really care. She was not going to get the chance to make me look like an absolute fool a third time. She had wanted me to call her last night, but when I called, not once, not twice, *but 3 times*, she couldn't or wouldn't come to the phone. I didn't need a house to fall on top on me to let me know when someone didn't care for me that much. I used to, but not now. Usually, Kelly had the same old unconcerned look she always had shown in the past, but this time, I saw some shock and maybe a little...hurt in her eyes?

NO WAY! She didn't and doesn't ever feel anything, and if she did, she'd be alright.

It looked like I was going to the prom by myself...

Thursday, April 3

I went to my locker before third period, and lo and behold, there was a note in it. *Oh no, Kelly, I'm not even going to read this note. You've already said your little speech twice before. This time I'm throwing this thing away...*

But then I looked closely at it, and it seemed to be real thick. I opened it, and this time, Kelly didn't write just one sentence; she wrote several sentences...almost three pages worth! During lunch time, I went to the library and read it. This was the condensed version:

Dear Cedric,

I want you to know I don't blame you for how you feel. But please *give me a chance to explain. First of all, I do have feelings for you, deep feelings for you. I know I don't show them but I do like you, a lot. I just am afraid if I show my feelings too strongly I'm going to wind up getting hurt, and I don't want that to happen. But I also don't want to lose you because you are a very nice and cute guy and you are a gentleman. I know I have funny ways and I know I've hurt you in the past, and I'm sorry for that. I hope you forgive me because I do want to go with you and I do want us to go to the prom together. I have never felt this strongly about a guy before, but there's something about you I just can't get over. I want us to get to know each other better and hopefully, we'll understand each other better and our relationship will grow into something nice.*

I can't believe I'm actually writing this, but I think I'm falling in love with you.

I really hope you forgive me. If you don't, I understand.

Kelly

I read it, re-read it, re-read it again, then re-read it one more time. I was shocked and surprised. Obviously, Kelly had written words even she thought she'd never write, and expressed her hidden feelings. I was touched, to say the very least. I had always felt there was something between us, some things that had been unsaid, a certain kind of attraction that didn't exist between me and no other girl, and I think all of that was finally beginning to rise to the surface because now, Kelly felt the same thing.

Kelly came into the library and talked to me after I read her note, and after some apologizing from both of us and some bonding of our feelings, we both realized that there *was* something between us and that, maybe, it *was* meant to be.

Friday, April 4

Kelly and I just about spent the whole day together (when we weren't in our various classes), either walking together or sitting close together, and talking as if we'd never been apart. Today I also gave Kelly something I'd been saving for the right moment and right person: I gave her my class ring on a silver chain for her to wear, as a symbol of our relationship. And yes, she wore it every day. I had never seen her this happy or this talkative. And I liked it. I think we sent a message today. All questions had been answered.

Tuesday, April 8

"Hey, Cedric! Come over here!"

Channeling my inner Curt, I mumbled to myself, "*Oh <bleep>.*"

I had decided to eat in the cafeteria for a change, and you all know what that meant.

Hello, Round Table.

I tried to pretend I didn't hear them, but it was fruitless.

"Cedric, I know you hear us calling you! Come here!" *Yeah, Joyce. I can hear you,* I was thinking. *Heck, they probably heard you in New Mexico.*

I hoped they wouldn't keep me too long because 1. I didn't like being away from Kelly too long. And, 2. I was actually hungry for a change.

"Yeah? What do ya'll want?"

Robrina said, "Oooo, look at him. He's glowing. You can tell he's happy about something."

Wendy spoke: "Yeah, he and Kelly just got back together. And from what I hear, she really has the hots for him."

I wondered briefly how they heard and know so much. Then Joyce said, "Uh-huh. Traci, girlfriend, you're outta luck. He done forgot all about <u>you</u>." I looked at Traci. She didn't think this was too funny. I was about to say I had forgotten about Traci back on Valentines' Day when Devin gave her those roses, when Joyce, who'd obviously say anything, asked me a different question: "Are you and Kelly going to do "it" after the prom?"

Wendy, Robrina, and Diana giggled. Of course, Traci still wasn't smiling. I don't know why; Sometimes she had a boyfriend, and sometimes she didn't. This must've been one of the "sometimes she didn't" times. Strangely, neither was Chandra. I was detecting a small level of jealousy and it was surprising to me. I turned red. I knew what they were talking about, but I pretended ignorance.

"Do what? What are you talking about?"

"You know what we're talking about, Cedric!" Robrina shot back.

"Don't play stupid! Are you going to '*do the do*' next Friday night?" Wendy and Diana giggled and laughed a little harder.

"I've gotta go," I said, not wanting to carry this kind of conversation with them.

"HEY!" Joyce fairly hollered, "I want to KNOW!"

Then suddenly came a strangely subdued voice: "Really, it's none of our business." *Was that Chandra speaking?*

"Yeah," said Traci, "leave him alone and let him go eat." *What?* I was stunned to the point where I couldn't move. *Is that Traci saying that?* Traci looked as though she were tired. I almost couldn't believe it.

Joyce and Robrina couldn't believe it, either. "What!? Don't y'all want to know if Cedric is going to make Kelly...uh, real happy?" Robrina asked as she looked at Traci and Chandra.

"Shoot! I'm not afraid to say it," Joyce was about to let loose, "I want to know if they're going to..."

"JOYCE!" Wendy shouted.

"...or not!"

"Cedric, you go ahead and go eat. We don't want to get in your business," said Chandra.

"Speak for yourself," muttered Joyce, whose brain and mouth were definitely in the gutter right now.

This was getting interesting. The Round Table was actually in disagreement about something. I almost didn't care if my french fries and chicken nuggets were getting cold right now.

"I think somebody's jealous," said Robrina, looking at Traci.

"I don't have anything to be jealous about. I just don't feel like hearing all that," said Traci, shooting Robrina a somewhat dirty look.

As the group started to argue, I walked away and didn't look back. Yep, message sent and received.

Thursday, April 17

A meeting was called today of all the seniors concerning the prom (tomorrow!) and early preparations for graduation. I sat next to Kelly, and on the other side of me, Devin sat next to Pamela Zaire, supposedly his date for the prom. I had already ordered and picked up my tux, and as far as driving went, the prom was to be held outside of Longview at this ballroom, so I figured it would be best if one of my parents drove us there instead. Again, as nervous as I was going to be, this would not be a good time to have a wreck. We were going to have pictures taken, so I ordered those also, so basically, I was ready for the prom.

Kelly and I had also been working on a class project for her computer math class together since I had taken the course the year before. I had a computer at home, so she was going to come by Monday so we could do some more work on it. We would be out-of-school that day. All and all, it was going to be an extra-long and extra-interesting weekend. I was looking forward to it in more ways than one...

CHAPTER 18

Prom Night 1986

Friday, April 18, 1986

The day went by quickly at school. My allergies had been acting up a little bit, but that wasn't going to stop me today. I couldn't wait for school to end, and when it finally did, I rode the bus home thinking of the night which was to be. Not even Flower-child, who was sitting next to me, could pierce my concentration.

When we arrived home, I didn't eat any supper; I just went and laid down and tried to take a nap. Of course, I couldn't, so I just laid there and thought good thoughts about Kelly and me. At 6 p.m., I got up and started getting ready. I took a bath, brushed my teeth, combed my hair, and put on the deodorant, powder and cologne. I wasn't leaving anything to chance. I got out my white tuxedo, shirt, and pants, with a maroon bow-tie and sash. I inspected every part for stains, holes, etc. and found none (but of course), and I carefully put everything on and made sure everything looked immaculate. I combed my hair once more then finally stepped out of the bathroom. It's a good thing we had two bathrooms; I was in there an hour and a half. It was like I was getting ready to play and sang *Sharp Dressed Man* by *ZZ Top*, one of my favorite songs at the time. Of course, my momma straightened a few things out herself on me, and then she wanted me to take some pictures. Flower stood nearby, making faces at me, but she was not going to break my concentration. I took the pictures with an air of confidence; finally, we got ready to leave.

"Have fun, big brother. Don't dance too hard," Flower said.

"Yeah, later." I walked out to the car and got in the passengers' side. I knew that some of my classmates were driving themselves and their dates to the prom for various "macho" reasons, but this time I was glad Momma was driving us to the prom because I knew I would've been too nervous to drive. This was pressure enough.

Speaking of pressure, when we arrived at Kelly's house, I started feeling really nervous for the first time all day. I almost wanted to forget about the whole thing and take off running. I tried to calm myself down as I got out of the car and walked towards Kelly's door. *You can do this*, I told myself. *Piece of cake*. Still, I was shaking a little bit as I went and rang the doorbell. One of Kelly's sisters answered the door and let me in, and as I looked around, it seemed that all of Kelly's family with the exception of Kelly and her mom were all sitting in the living room. Kelly's dad greeted me warmly, "How's it going, son? Ready for the big night?" "Uh, y-yes sir." *Why did I have to stutter? Sure, I was.* Kelly's three younger sisters looked at me smiling and grinning the whole time. I was fixing to start sweating when suddenly Kelly came into the room, followed by her mom.

"Oh my God," I said to myself.

Kelly looked beautiful! I almost fainted from the sight of her. Her hair was curled and done neatly and it fit her sparkling face and eyes perfectly. In fact, I didn't know her eyes were so pretty because she usually wore glasses most of the time. Her makeup looked to be done by a pro, and her white, shiny dress fit her figure like a hand to a glove. She smiled, walked up to me, and said, "Well, what do you think?" I tried to clear my throat and tried not to sound stupid: "It's...it's...you look beautiful." I was staring so much I almost forgot I had bought her a corsage to wear. "This is for you," I said, and I started pinning the corsage to her dress hoping I wasn't touching her inappropriately in front of her parents. The thought of that was making me even more nervous in the process. At that moment, however, her parents were so happy for their daughter and me that they weren't noticing too much of anything. But somehow I got it pinned without sticking her or myself. We took some more pictures, then we got ready to go. The prom was to start at 9 p.m., so I told Kelly's parents we'd be back by 12, they said, OK, and we walked out to the car. My mom and her parents greeted each other as I opened the door for Kelly, let her get in, closed the door, then I walked to the other side and got in. We both sat in the back, of course. After final goodbyes, my mom drove off and we were headed for the PROM. This year, the prom was being held a few miles outside of Longview at the SPJST Ballroom, and we had to get on the interstate to get there. Again, I was thankful I wasn't driving, because not too long ago Daddy had taken me to practice my driving in his truck, and he told me to get on the interstate. Needless to say, that was a terror-filled 15 minutes worth of driving practice. The truck's steering wheel felt like it was loose, and I felt like I was going to run (speed) off the road any second. Again, I was glad to be driven to the prom. Kelly didn't seem to mind either.

We arrived there about fifteen minutes early, so after Kelly and I got out of the car and my mom left, we went in and there were only three other couples who had gotten there before us. Kelly went to the restroom to freshen up, and I watched as KFRO, the radio station which was going to be broadcasting live from our prom, finished getting everything set up.

There were balloons everywhere, and everything had been decorated Lobo green. It looked nice. Kelly came out of the restroom and sat next to me, and we talked for a little bit until the photographers said they were ready to start taking couples' pictures. Kelly and I got into line; by this time, there were like ten couples ahead of us and more arriving by the minute behind us. My anxiety reached its peak as we stood in line, and I thought, *Please don't let me pass out.* When it came time for us to take pictures, Kelly put her arm around me, and my nervousness left me, just like that. I put my arm around her and we held hands, then we took our pictures. I knew they were going to look good.

By this time, almost everybody had arrived, and the music was already playing. I noticed that the dance floor was awfully slick, so I decided not to take too many chances on it trying to dance to some of the faster tunes. In fact, one of Kelly's friends asked if he could dance with her first, and I didn't mind, since it was a fast song, and I was trying to get up a little more bravery to go out there and keep from falling. While they were dancing, I went and spoke to Dave, who had arrived in a black tux and was looking real natty.

"What's up, Dave? I see you made it." He smiled.

"Yeah, I figured I might as well come out and bust a move. You come with Kelly?"

"Yeah. She's already out there dancing. My goodness, she looks good."

I was beginning to think I better hurry up and start dancing with her before some guy tried to take her. Dave looked out towards the dance floor. "You're right. She looks lovely. I better find my date so we can go get our pictures taken. Later, 'gator."

Later on, my twin brother finally arrived, and he looked to be hiding in a corner with some other friends of ours laughing the whole time. After dancing with Kelly for a while, I went up to him.

"So, Mr. Devin Micheals, you finally decided to grace our prom with your presence."

"Yeah, I figured it wouldn't be much of a prom without the man to liven up things." Devin was feeling unusually cocky.

"So, who's your date?" I asked.

"I didn't bring one."

"Say what? You're lying. What about Pamela? Valecia? Or Traci?" I still hadn't forgotten Valentines' Day.

"I didn't come with anyone. I wasn't real sure if I was coming to the prom. So I didn't tell anyone I was going to take them out. I really didn't decide until 9 o'clock. Then when I did, I had to come by myself, which is better anyway."

I couldn't see how it could get any better than dating the girl of your dreams but then again Devin always did like to throw curves into things.

"Whatever," I said, "I need to get back to Kelly."

"Yeah, I seen y'all out there making eyes at each other. By the way, Ced E., I didn't know you could dance. You were getting down out there."

"You need to get out there and dance with somebody instead of standing here laughing at everybody," I told him, "I'll see you later."

Not only did I see those two, but I saw and spoke to Micheal and his date, his girlfriend from Dallas; Annette, who seemed to be a little jealous I was with Kelly; the Round Table gang, who still wanted the answers to their obscene questions; Curtis and some of his buddies; Ben Stevens, the Dennis Boys, George Tracy, Ron Lane, and some of Kelly's friends: Lorraine, Tanja, Leslie, and the only other girl I danced with at the prom besides Kelly, Katrina Lee.

After I got through talking to Dave and Devin, the song that was playing ended and another song was about to be played, so I was walking over towards Kelly, who was coming towards me, and we met and both went out to the dance floor and danced to Janet Jackson's *What Have You Done For Me Lately* and *Nasty Boys*. I made a mental reminder to myself that I was going to have to go get that tape the next time I went to the mall. I started off a little nervous at first, but I got into the swing of things and did pretty good for someone who's pretty average on a dance floor. In fact, my classmates were impressed. Kelly danced better than me, of course, and though we were both kind of shy around each other initially, we were both coming out of that rather rapidly. As the time passed on, we went from glancing at each other to just staring into each other's eyes. The slow dances were particularly satisfying. I had never slow danced with anyone else before, and this was actually my first time doing so. Slow-dancing with Kelly was like going to Heaven. The mood was perfect; the lights were down and the only lighting there was were the candles lit at the tables. Kelly and I slow-danced to the music of Lisa-Lisa, the Force MDs, and Mtume, and every time we slow-danced (which was like four or five times) we got closer and closer. In fact, I had make-up stains on my shoulder that I didn't even notice until later. Pretty soon it had gotten to the point we were oblivious to everything and everyone around us; we were either looking into each other's eyes, or we were holding each other really close as we danced.

After we finally came off the dance floor and sat down at a table, we talked for a while, then I kind of motioned for her to sit closer to me, which she most definitely did. If she had sat any closer she would've been in my lap, and I don't think it would have minded. I put my arm around her, she leaned against me, and as the candles burned brightly, it was clear that there was romance in the air. Other friends of ours approached us and spoke to us, but it was obvious we weren't paying much attention, and for the most part, we sat together alone as I whispered into her ear. (It was loud in the building, you know.)

Finally, at a little bit after 11 p.m., Kelly and I decided we were ready to leave, so we told our goodbyes and went outside where my mom was waiting. I did my gentlemanly duties, and we left and headed out to eat at Denny's. Strangely, even though I hadn't ate since lunch time at school, I still wasn't hungry (Kelly wasn't, either) and all we could do was sit at the table, play with our food, and look at each other. "I know I've said this too many times tonight, but you look gorgeous. I can't stop looking at you." I felt as though in a trance. She was feeling the same way and said so. I knew I wanted to kiss her, but when would be the right time? I had kissed her on her ear a few times while I was "whispering" to her at the prom, but I was thinking about a real kiss, like the kind one saw in movies. I didn't really want to do it in front of my mom, but I probably had no choice. We left the restaurant after only taking about three bites between us and headed for Kelly's home. Suddenly, I started feeling nervous again. *This was it. The goodbye kiss. Please don't let me blow it.* But then when we turned into Kelly's driveway at about 5 minutes until 12, her front door opened and her whole family came outside including some aunts, uncles, and grandparents. There was no way I was going to kiss Kelly goodbye in front of them *and* my momma. I was a little disappointed, and so was Kelly, but I told her goodnight and goodbye and she told me she'd see me Monday...at my house.

Aftermath of the Greatest Prom Ever: Monday, April 21st

I had told my mom that Kelly was coming over and that we were going to work on her Computer Math project together. (My dad was at work.) For some reason, my momma didn't believe me and she and my sister got ready to go to the store around the same time (1 p.m.) Kelly was supposed to come over. I didn't want Kelly to think no one was here after coming almost across town, so I tried to delay Momma a bit, but she and my sister left before Kelly came over.

"If she comes over, go ahead and let her in...but I don't think she's coming," my momma said as she backed out of the driveway.

Five minutes after they left, Kelly and her mother drove up.

I went outside and told Kelly's mom I was the only one at home and that my momma would be back shortly, and she went on ahead and dropped Kelly off and left.

Talk about things falling into place.

"Now, where were we?" Kelly asked, as we went into my room.

"I think we were to the part where I was supposed to kiss you good night," I said.

"Well, come here then," said Kelly.

Our goodnight kiss turned into a virtual lip lock, as we really got closer to each other. We weren't thinking about no project or worrying about nosy family members; we were two teenagers in love.

We stopped before things got too far out of hand and when we heard my momma and sister drive up. I will never forget the look on my momma's (as well as Flower-child's) face when she saw Kelly and I in my room together, working on the project. She was shocked and really didn't know how to react. "Hello," I said, feeling strangely confident. A little more than dumbfounded, Momma gave me a crazy look. Finally, she reacted by being real nice to Kelly and making sure we were comfortable as we studied and worked. Flower-child went into her room, left the door open, and pretended to be reading a book while the whole time watching what was going on. After a while, though, I closed my door and Kelly and I had a little privacy.

Later, when Daddy came home, and my momma told him what was going on, he didn't appear too shocked or too concerned. He spoke to Kelly, then went and took a nap. (If it had been Flower-child, however, he probably would have exploded.) Finally, Kelly's mom came to pick her up, we told each other bye (with a small amount of guilty smiling and grinning), and they left. Of course, Momma reiterated that she had really believed that Kelly wasn't going to come over and that it surprised her greatly that she had. She also couldn't believe I'd let Kelly in the house without anyone else being there. *Why not?* I thought to myself. *She said I could, so I did.* She wanted to know did anything happen before Flower and her came back home.

"Of course not, Momma. We just studied."

As long as I live, I'll never forget that weekend.

CHAPTER 19

The End

Thursday, May 1, 1986

I probably should have seen it coming. I probably should have known better than to think something like this would last forever (or, at least a month or two). I probably should have listened to everyone who said I was making a mistake. I probably should have never left Abilene.

How did the saying go? Fool me once, shame on you; fool me twice, shame on me. Fool me thrice, shame on...Well, there was enough shame to go around for all of North America.

Again.

Kelly did it to me again.

And this time, like a Lawrence Taylor coming in from the blindside and nailing a helpless quarterback who doesn't see, hear, or smell him coming, this came from nowhere.

And like the little old lady in the commercial, I *almost* didn't get back up.

Things had been going well since the greatest prom ever. Kelly and I had been to each others' homes visiting, we talked on the phone every evening, as well as spending time together at school, and we seemed to make a great couple. She wasn't acting like she had acted at the beginning of the school year, where she was seemingly unfriendly and very distant-like. This time, she was the total opposite. She wrote me another note the week before telling me again how much she loved me and how much she enjoyed the prom and that she couldn't wait for us to go out again. *Call it an engagement*, she wrote. I was thinking, *She is really in love with me.* And I was definitely feeling the same way about her. I wasn't talking to or thinking about no one else but Kelly. Traci? *Who's she?* Annette? *Annette who?* Round Table? *What's a Round table? Never heard of them.* I really believed in being faithful to a person because I would want to be treated the same. And I didn't feel that Kelly and I had any problems in that regard.

Now, I wondered.

Kelly had come by my house the previous Friday and we finished her computer math project. No, this time my family didn't leave. Things were still normal between us at that time. We didn't see or talk to each other over the weekend, then that Monday, at school, I saw her and she wasn't looking too well. I asked her how was she doing, and she told me she wasn't feeling too good. I felt it was one of those "women" things, so I didn't nag her about it or anything, and the day went by smoothly.

Tuesday was more of the same, then yesterday (Wednesday), our prom pictures came back. They were so <u>beautiful</u>! Kelly looked stunning in the pictures. I immediately had flashbacks to the greatest prom ever. After picking them up, I took Kelly her pictures that evening. She still seemed to be under the weather, so I didn't stay too long. It started raining that day and the evening felt dreary, and for a second, I felt like something was wrong but I chalked it up to the bad weather and forgot about it.

Until 1:45 today.

I had skipped lunch and gone to the library to study for a test I was having in Calculus the next day. Kelly, who usually met me at the library at that time so we could walk to our classes together, came up to me and handed me a note, then quickly left before I could say anything. I thought this was kind of strange and at first I was almost afraid to read it. But then I thought, *If it had been a bad note she would've stuck it in my locker.* All her "good" notes she had handed to me in person, so then I thought, *Shoot, I'm worrying for nothing.*

I opened the note and read it:

Dear Cedric:

> I'm sorry, but I don't think we should go together any longer. I will give you your ring back to you tomorrow before first period. It's nothing personal, but I just don't think we belong together.
>
> Kelly

I stared at the note, put it in my notebook and walked to my fifth period class in a daze. I went to my seat, and then took the note out and read it again during class. Usually I'd be tripping out with Micheal, Rayzell, and Ben, but today I was like a deaf-mute, and my friends noticed. They, especially Micheal, tried to get me to talk about it, but I was still in shock and didn't feel like talking. Then I read it again during sixth period Spanish. Not even Curt could snap me out of my funk. I didn't see Kelly the rest of the day, which was just as well, for I probably wasn't and wouldn't have been in the right frame of mind to talk to her anyway. The words of Flower-child haunted me: *I hope she's not using you.* She had always thought it strange that someone who, at first, had wanted nothing to do with me could do a 180 and then act(?) as if they couldn't live without me all of a sudden. It didn't help that all this had occurred the way it did. Now, with the prom being over with and her receiving her pictures and her project being finished, now we were *finished*. Coincidence? Maybe, but I doubt it. Had I been used? I hoped not. But it certainly looked that way.

Friday, May 2

It had never failed to happen. As soon as I started feeling something for someone, I got dropped or rejected. I didn't know if it was supposed to be the other way around or not, but all I knew was that I did not feel too good about myself. Why and how did I let things like this happen to me? Was I supposed to be without feelings like some of the other guys I know who seemingly have a different girlfriend every couple of weeks? Why did I even *want* a girlfriend? (Well, the answer to *that* question is kind of obvious.) But seriously, I began to doubt myself as to being able to have a decent relationship with a girl and wondered if the whole business was worth it. Sure, I had enjoyed being with Kelly (and Annette, for that matter, earlier in the year for a couple of weeks), but if it was going to last only a few weeks, then it wasn't worth it. I wasn't a playboy or a Casanova (or even a "Don Juan"); I was my own person, and if girls couldn't like me for myself, then I didn't need them. Let me rephrase that: I didn't need a girlfriend to live; I wanted to have a meaningful relationship with a girl in the future. But I wasn't going to allow myself to be used in any kind of way again. It was going to make for a lot of lonely days in the future, but at least I wouldn't be questioning myself or feeling the hurt and anger I felt on May 1st, 1986.

CHAPTER 20

Graduation '86 (Finally)

The Month of May, 1986:

On Friday, April 25th, a letter arrived in the mail which stated: *Congratulations! You are now a Lumberjack! You have been accepted to attend Stephen F. Austin State University.*

I was happy, for it meant I'd be going to school with Lawrence for the next four years and as a result, college was probably not going to be so bad after all. I told L.C. the news the following Sunday at church and he was ecstatic.

"That's alright!" he said.

"Me and you, we're going to turn SFA out!" I said, "yeah, call us the 'Dynamic Duo'."

L.C. then went a step further (or backward, however you want to look at it): "Or, the 'Lumberjack Duo'," L.C. and I laughed at the sound of that. But first, there was the matter of graduating from high school that needed to be taken care of first.

After my break-up with Kelly, the rest of the month of May was spent preparing for Graduation and realizing we had one more month where we all would be going to school together and seeing one another for the final time. My grades had been great the entire year (I had made the honor roll in all the six-week periods except the fourth), so I wasn't in any danger of failing any courses and being unable to graduate with the rest of my class. Our graduating class was going to be HUGE--370+graduates, and I hoped all my friends and classmates would get to participate in the ceremonies and not be held back by grades or anything else for that matter.

There was also the matter of getting fitted for the cap and gown. My cap and gown fit me the first time I tried it on, and when I looked at myself in the mirror, that's when I first realized that, *Hey, I'm fixing to be graduating from LHS. I won't be in high school no more.* I kind of choked up a little bit as I thought about that, but then it was back to reality. I had applied for some scholarships to help me pay for college, but I hadn't received any at that point, so I had that to worry about also.

I also had to get my invitations mailed and sent out (or given out), and get my autograph/memory book signed by most of my friends before graduation. That was a chore in itself, for by this time I had so many friends and acquaintances that I didn't want to forget anyone who I'd known over a long period of time or a short period of time, or even casual friends who I'd seen and spoken to every now and then. I really needed three or four autograph books to get all the signatures I wanted to get

There was one very special signature I got from a person I would never, ever forget, and that was from my fifth grade teacher back when I was at Jodie McClure. Miss Stone was in her first year of teaching back then, so I was a member of the very first class she'd ever taught. Being a teacher was and is probably more difficult than a lot of your so-called "tough jobs". (Believe me, I know!), and probably as in any other occupation, one's first year at something is usually the most difficult year. My fifth grade class wasn't the best-acting class in the world, but with the exception of three or four kids who were in there to do nothing more than disrupt things, it was a pretty good class. This was also my first and last year at Jodie McClure, and being the new kid for like the hundredth time in my life at that time had left me somewhat depressed. But I wasn't depressed too long because Miss Stone identified with me as far as being new was concerned, and she didn't let things or situations get her down and she let me know I shouldn't either. She almost always had a smile on her face, and though she was nice (Definitely the nicest teacher I've ever had), she was also fair and stern when she had to be. She was the first teacher I could go up and talk to about anything, and she was this way with almost the whole class. Though we were little kids at the time, she could communicate and relate to us real well, whether we were black or white. She was and still is the best teacher I've ever had.

When I went over to my old school and told her I was graduating and that I wanted to thank her for her help towards this goal, she told me she was very proud of me, and for some reason, at that moment, that meant more to me than if my parents had said the same thing. Thank you, Miss Stone.

Monday, May 26, 1986

We were out-of-school today for Memorial Day, so I spent the day studying for my final (for real) exams and thinking of the many classmates I'd probably not see anymore after Graduation Day this Thursday. After about 30 minutes of this, I got up, went outside and got on my bike and rode to Devin's house. I passed by Shelia's house on the way there, and almost predictably, she came running out the door and chased me halfway down the block calling me every name in the book. But unless she was Flo-Jo or Carl Lewis or somebody, she wasn't gonna catch me. As I sped through the neighborhood, I imagined what it was going to be like riding through Nacogdoches like this instead of Longview. Then a thought came to my mind which I was probably going to repeat many times in the future: *I've got to get me a car.* And: *I need to hurry up and get my drivers' license. Soon.*

Anyway, when I got to Devin's, he was already outside mowing his yard and was halfway done with it when I came riding up in his driveway. He turned off the mower and walked towards me as I parked and sat up on my bike.

"What's up, little man?" he asked, "enjoying the day off?"

"I'm just chillin'," I said, "getting ready for the big day. You ready for it?"

"About as ready as I'll ever be. How about you?"

"I guess so. By the way, there's something I've been meaning to ask you."

"Shoot."

"How in the world did you get elected 'Playboy of the Year'?"

Bear in mind that this was not an official award voted on by the senior class or by LHS period; this had been something done by the girls in Devin's 5th period English class which, incidentally, consisted of mostly cheerleaders, Viewettes, and the creamest of the crop, Miss Calacia. In fact, Calacia was the one who gave him the award. And you can bet the farm that Devin's head grew bigger than Russia when that happened.

There had been other "unofficial awards" given that day such as "Loudest Girl," "Craziest Guy," "Most Un-Athletic," "Biggest Behind," and that sort of thing, but Devin had obviously gotten the most sought-after award. And I wondered how.

"Well, you know how it is...when you're hot, you're hot, and when you're not, you're not. Right?" Devin looked at me smugly for a response. I just looked at him. Then he continued: "I mean, Calacia knew what she was doing when she handed me, the Man himself, the most coveted of all awards, even more so than "Mr. Lobo," the Playboy of the Year Award. And then gave yours truly a very nice hug. And let me say this: It was a great moment." He smiled a huge smile at the memory.

"Well, you know if I had been in that class, you'd have came in second place," I said half-seriously, "that's a fact."

Devin laughed and said,"Uh-huh. Sure. All I got to say to you is, '*ifs and buts, candy and nuts.*'"

We both laughed. I wished Devin were going to SFA, too, at that moment. I knew we would have turned the place inside-out. We were still domino *and* basketball partners and there were probably victims to be had in Deep East Texas, too. Still, he didn't deserve to be "Playboy of the Year." Not yet, anyway.

Further down the street Devin lived on, I saw my cousin, Kellie Anders. I stopped and talked to her. "Remember when we were both at East Ward Elementary back in the first and second grades?" She asked. "Those were the good ol' days." They sure were. Kellie had always been fun to be around, and I can still remember us playing together when we were little kids and us going together along with her little brother and my little sister and sitting in Santa Claus' lap at Sears back then. And even though we kind of lost touch when I moved away and started going to different schools, when we both arrived at LHS, she was still the same friendly person she had always been. I'll never forget how she took up for me when we were in the 9th grade just entering high school when some so-called "friends" were harassing me. "I got your back, cuz," she told me even though she might have been four feet tall at the time. And I was probably four feet four inches myself at the time. I wasn't so chauvinistic not to appreciate that, and she may have been called "Little Kel," but her heart was bigger than the state we lived in, and that's saying something. (Oh, and by the way, Kel, thanks for telling my momma the time I got in trouble and got paddled for cutting in line back when we were in the first grade. I know it's been some years but I really appreciated you telling her that, especially when I wasn't going to. My behind appreciated it, also. Wait, that wasn't you? Ok, my bad.)

Perhaps the funniest final moment occurred during 6th period Spanish, and yes, it involved Curt. I had brought a small tape-recorder to school to record the final words of some of my classmates as we neared the end of school. As I recall, Devin again bragged about being Playboy of the Year ("Hugh would be proud of me!"), Dave talked about going to SMU and testing the machine-gun theory there ("Maybe it ought to be a class."), the Round Table talked their normal crazy-talk ("How many girls are you going to go after this summer?"--except they didn't quite put it that way), and others just spoke on getting ready for the finals and preparing for graduation. But no one put it more eloquently and more directly than my man Curt. As we quietly studied during class, Curt took the tape recorder and made a short speech. Here was the condensed and (very) censored version in his very own words:

"Three more days and I'm so glad. Can't wait to get out of this <bleeping> <bleep>house. This has been a <bleep> year. Really, this has been a bunch of <bleep>. Makes me want to <bleep>. Tired of this <bleepity-bleep> school. Know what I <bleeping> mean? <Bleep><Bleeping><Bleep>!"

Those of us who heard him as he half-whispered these words into the tape-recorder were shaking to keep from laughing out loud. Then, of course, he had to attack Pookie one final time.

"By the way, Pookie is a <bleep> transvestite!"

We came unglued with laughter.

The final exams were, to say the least, anti-climatic. The hardest exam was Calculus (as always) and I just wanted to pass that one. The rest were pretty easy. (See what happens when you study?) By the end of the day, it was official: I was going to be graduating from LHS and receiving my diploma. I was very happy and very relieved that the high-school experience was nearly over. I didn't have a girlfriend to share my joy and relief with (it would've been nice, but oh well), but at that moment, I didn't particularly care. Like Curt, I was ready to graduate and get away. I had gotten everyone I knew to sign my books and I traded name cards with most of my friends. I had turned in all of my books, had no fines, library or otherwise, and had cleaned out my locker like yesterday. So I was ready.

We had graduation practice today out on the field. It probably lasted no more than 45 minutes, but felt more like two or three hours to me. Let me explain: We came out onto the football field and they arranged us in alphabetical order according to our last names. Then they had us march to our seats and stand there. It was very hot outside, and for some stupid reason, my momma thought we were supposed to dress up for practice as if it were actually Graduation. And she basically made me wear this hot, long-sleeved black shirt along with khaki pants. Needless to say, I was HOT in more ways than one. Everyone else had on tank-tops, shorts, flip-flops, etc., while I was dressed as if I were going to church in ten-degree weather. *Oh well*, I thought, *come August I won't have to worry about things like this happening anymore.*

Graduation Night:

As the music started playing and my classmates and I marched across the field for the final time to our seats, I finally felt the sadness of the moment. Suddenly I realized I wasn't going to see many of my classmates and friends ever again after this night. There probably should've been a sign resembling a city limits sign which said, "LEAVING LONGVIEW HIGH SCHOOL--POPULATION 1,500." Some of us were going to move far, far away to different states and different countries; some of us were going to move elsewhere in Texas; and a few of us would probably continue to live in East Texas. But we would never be together like this again. We were each going to go our our separate ways and to our separate destinies, whether they be good or unfortunately for some, bad. It was sad to think about all this, but again, the saddest fact of all was that we, as a group, had spent our final day together at Longview High School. A lot of friendships were going to fade away and a lot of the camaraderie built up for four years would slowly disappear, also. Past relationships were going to become a footnote in time, and our going to and attending LHS would in time also become a memory. Strangely as I sat thinking on all of these things, I was no longer nervous. As our valedictorian (my buddy Dave) spoke, I sat thinking--wishing I could have one more day with Flower-child at school. Maybe even two. One more day to trip out with Devin, Dave, Curt, Mike, and all my other friends. To listen to them talk about girls, food, money, and school. One more day of Spanish class so I could laugh until the tears ran. One more football practice. One more time to sit with the Round Table. One more time to be "Little Stacy Wonderful". One more time to play dominoes in the field house. One more day to let Kelly, Annette, Traci, Randi, Vanessa, and Calacia know how I really felt about them (I guess). And of course, one more day of Calculus class. (Strike that.)

Then I realized it didn't all have to end on a sad note. Friendships would probably end, but there'd be others to take their place. And some friendships will probably never die anyway. Besides, aren't that what class reunions are for in the first place?

Finally, I heard my name announced over the loudspeaker, and as I walked across the stage and received my diploma, the sadness was permanently replaced by happiness, and I smiled at my family sitting in the stands and my family of classmates all around me.

I had finally GRADUATED.

Goodbye Longview High School.

Welcome to the Real World.

ABOUT THE AUTHOR

The author, Cedric Edwards is currently a high-school instructional assistant and inclusion teacher for Social Studies. He was born in Kittery, Maine (of all places) in 1968, and moved to Texas when he was but four months old. Therefore, he considers himself a Texan.

Cedric graduated from Longview High School in Longview, Texas in 1986 and attended Stephen F. Austin State University for a few years afterward. He is currently working towards his B.A. in Information Technology with a minor in General Business at SFA.

Cedric collects comic books and football cards as a hobby, enjoys working on the computer, watching football, playing dominoes and basketball, and spending time playing with his twin 3 year-old-grandchildren, Alijah and Aaliyah.

www.ingramcontent.com/pod-product-compliance
Lightning Source LLC
Chambersburg PA
CBHW071903290426
44110CB00013B/1258